Chef at Home

Complete Healthy Cookbook

Maurice B. Sundquist

CREAMS

APRICOT CREAMS.

1 pint of cream, the whites of 4 eggs, some apricot jam, 2 inches of vanilla pod, 1 dessertspoonful of castor sugar. Split the vanilla, put this and the sugar into the cream; whip this with the whites of eggs until stiff, then remove the vanilla. Place a good teaspoonful of apricot jam in each custard glass, and fill up with whipped cream.

BLACKBERRY CREAM.

1 quart of blackberries, sugar to taste, 1/2 pint of cream, white of 2 eggs. Mash the fruit gently, put it into a hair-sieve and allow it to drain. Sprinkle the fruit with sugar to make the juice drain more freely; whip the cream and mix with the juice.

CHOCOLATE CREAM.

1 quart of milk, 6 oz. of Allinson chocolate, 4 eggs, 1 tablespoonful of Allinson corn flour, essence of vanilla, sugar to taste. Dissolve the chocolate in a few tablespoonfuls of water, stirring it over the fire until a thick, smooth paste; add the milk, vanilla, and sugar. When boiling thicken the milk with the cornflour; remove the mixture from the fire to cool slightly, beat the eggs well, stir them into the thickened chocolate very gradually, and stir the whole over the fire, taking care not to allow it to boil When well thickened let the cream cool; serve in custard glasses or poured over sponge cakes or macaroons.

CHOCOLATE CREAM (French) (1).

Use the whites of 3 eggs to 2 large bars of chocolate; vanilla to taste. Break the chocolate in pieces, and melt it in a little enamelled saucepan with very little water; stir it quite smooth, and flavour with Allinson vanilla essence. Set the chocolate aside until quite cold, when it should be a smooth paste, and not too firm. Beat the whites of the eggs to a very stiff froth, and mix the chocolate with it, stirring both well together until the chocolate is well mixed with the froth. It the cream is not found sweet enough, add a little castor sugar. Serve in a glass dish. This is easily made, and very dainty.

CHOCOLATE CREAM (WHIPPED).

2 oz. of Allinson chocolate to 1/4 pint of cream, white of 1 egg. Dissolve the chocolate over the fire with 2 tablespoonfuls of water; let it get quite cold, and then mix it with the cream previously whipped stiff; this will not require any additional sugar.

EGG CREAM.

The yolks of 6 eggs, 1/2 pint of water, juice of 1 lemon, 2 oz. of sifted sugar, a little cinnamon. Beat up all the ingredients, put the mixture into a saucepan over a sharp fire, and whisk it till quite frothy, taking care not to let it boil; fill into glasses and serve at once.

LEMON CREAM.

The juice of 3 lemons and the rind of 1, 7 eggs, 6 oz. of sugar, 1 dessertspoonful of cornflour. Proceed exactly as in "Orange Cream."

MACAROON CREAM.

Pound 1-1/2 doz. macaroons, place in a bowl, add 1 or 2 spoonfuls of milk, and mix all to a smooth paste. Take a 6d. jar of cream, whip to a stiff froth. Lay a little of the macaroon paste roughly in the bottom of a glass dish, then 1 or 2 spoonfuls of the cream, more paste and cream, then cover with 1 spoonful of cream put on roughly.

ORANGE CREAM.

6 oranges, 1 lemon, 7 eggs, 4 to 6 oz. of sugar (according to taste), 1 dessertspoonful of cornflour, some water. Take the juice of the oranges and the juice and grated rind of the lemon. Add enough water to the fruit juice to make 1-1/2 pints of liquid; let this get hot, adding the sugar to it; mix the cornflour smooth with a spoonful of cold water, and thicken the fruit juice with it, letting it boil up for a minute, set aside and let it cool a little; beat the eggs well, and when the liquid has cooled mix them carefully in with it; return the whole over a gentle fire, keep stirring continually until the cream thickens, but take care not to let it boil, as this would curdle it. When cold, serve in custard glasses, or in a glass dish poured over macaroons.

RASPBERRY CREAM.

1 quart of raspberries, sugar to taste, 1/2 pint of cream. Proceed as in "Blackberry Cream."

RUSSIAN CREAM.

Lay 6 sponge cakes on a glass dish, and soak them with any fruit syrup; then add 1 pint of blancmange. When nearly cold cover the top with ratafia biscuits and decorate with angelica and cherries.

STRAWBERRY CREAM.

1 quart of strawberries, sugar to taste, 1/2 pint of cream. Proceed as in "Blackberry Cream."

SWISS CREAM.

1/2 pint of cream, 1/2 pint of milk, 1 tablespoonful of Allinson cornflour, 1/4 lb. of macaroons, 2 oz. of ratafias, vanilla, and sugar to taste. Put the cream and milk over the fire, adding a piece of vanilla 2 inches long, and sugar to taste; smooth the cornflour with a tablespoonful of cold milk, mix it with the milk and cream when nearly boiling, stir the mixture over the fire until it has thickened and let it simmer 2 minutes longer, always stirring; remove the vanilla, arrange the macaroons and ratafias on a shallow glass dish, let the cream cool a little, then pour it over the biscuits and serve cold. This makes a delicious dish.

WHIPPED CREAMS.

Quantity of good thick cream according to requirement. The white of 1 egg to 1/4 pint. Whip it well with a whisk or fork until it gets quite thick; in hot weather it should be kept on ice or standing in another basin with cold water, as the cream might curdle. Add sugar to taste and whatever flavouring might be desired, this latter giving the cream its name. When whipped cream is used to pour over sweets, &c., flavour it with stick vanilla; a piece 1 inch long is sufficient for 1/2 pint of cream; it must be split and as much as possible of the little grains in it rubbed into the cream.

CUSTARDS

ALMOND CUSTARD.

1 quart of milk, 6 eggs, 1 dessertspoonful of Allinson cornflour, 1 wineglassful of rosewater, sugar to taste, 1/2 lb. ground almonds. Boil the milk with the sugar and almonds; smooth the cornflour with the rosewater and stir it into the boiling milk, let it boil up for a minute. Beat up the eggs, leaving out 3 of the whites of the eggs, which are to be beaten to a stiff froth. Let the milk cool a little, then stir in the eggs very gradually, taking care not to curdle them; stir over the fire until the custard is nearly boiling, then let it cool, stirring occasionally; pour it into a glass dish, and pile the whipped whites of the eggs on the top of the custard just before serving.

BAKED APPLE CUSTARD.

8 large apples, moist sugar to taste, half a teacupful of water and the juice of half a lemon, 1 pint of custard made with Allinson custard powder. Peel, cut and core the apples and put into a lined saucepan with the water, sugar, and lemon juice, stew till tender and rub through a sieve; when cold put the fruit at the bottom of a pie-dish and pour the custard over, grate a little nutmeg over the top, bake lightly, and serve cold.

BAKED CUSTARD.

1 quart of milk, 6 eggs, sugar, and flavouring to taste. Heat the milk until nearly boiling, sweeten it with sugar, and add any kind of flavouring. Whip up the eggs, and mix them carefully with the hot milk. Pour the custard into

a buttered pie-dish, and bake it in a moderately hot oven until set. If the milk and eggs are mixed cold and then baked the custard goes watery; it is therefore important to bear in mind that the milk should first be heated. Serve with stewed fruit.

CARAMEL CUSTARD.

1-1/2 pints of milk, 4 eggs, 1 dessertspoonful of sugar, 1/2 lemon and 4 oz. of castor sugar for caramel. Put the dry castor sugar into an enamelled saucepan and let it melt and turn a rich brown over the fire, stirring all the time. When the sugar is melted and browned stir into it about 2 tablespoonfuls of hot water, and the juice of 1/2 lemon. Then pour the caramel into a mould or cake-tin, and let it run all round the sides of the tin. Meanwhile heat the milk near boiling-point, and add the vanilla and sugar. Whip up the eggs, stir carefully into them the hot milk, so as not to curdle the eggs. Then pour the custard into the tin on the caramel and stand the tin in a larger tin with hot water, place it in the oven, and bake in a moderately hot oven for about 20 minutes or until the custard is set. Allow it to get cold, turn out, and serve.

CARAMEL CUP CUSTARD (French).

Make the custard as in the recipe for "Cup Custard." Take 4 oz. of castor sugar; put it over a brisk fire in a small enamelled saucepan, keep stirring it until quite melted and a rich brown. Then cautiously add 2 tablespoonfuls of boiling water, taking care not to be scalded by the spluttering sugar. Gradually stir the caramel into the hot custard. Let it cool, and serve in custard glasses.

CUP CUSTARD.

6 whole eggs or 10 yolks of eggs, 1 quart of milk, sugar and vanilla to taste. Beat the eggs well while the milk is being heated. Use vanilla pods to flavour—they are better than the essence, which is alcoholic; split a piece of the pod 3 or 4 inches long, and let it soak in the milk for 1 hour before it is set over the fire, so as to extract the flavour from the vanilla. Sweeten the milk and let it come nearly to boiling-point. Carefully stir the milk into the beaten eggs, adding only a little at a time, so as not to curdle the eggs. When all is mixed, pour the custard into a jug, which should be placed in a saucepanful of boiling water. Keep stirring the custard with a wooden spoon, and as soon as the custard begins to coat the spoon remove the saucepan from the fire, and continue stirring the custard until it is well thickened. In doing as here directed there is no risk of the custard curdling, for directly the water ceases to boil it cannot curdle the custard, although it is hot enough to finish thickening it. If the milk is nearly boiling when mixed with the eggs, the custard will only take from 5 to 10 minutes to finish. When the custard is done place the jug in which it was made in a bowl of cold water, stir it often while cooling to prevent a skin forming on the top. Remove the vanilla pod and pour the custard into glasses. Should the custard be required very thick, 8 eggs should be used, or the milk can first be thickened with a dessertspoonful of Allinson cornflour before mixing it with the 6 eggs. This is an excellent plan; it saves eggs, and the custard tastes just as rich as if more eggs were used. Serve in custard glasses, or in a glass dish.

CUSTARD (ALLINSON).

1 pint of milk or cream, 2 oz. of lump sugar and 1 packet of Allinson custard powder. Put the contents of the packet into a basin and mix to a smooth, thin paste with about 2 tablespoonfuls of the milk; boil the remainder of milk with the sugar, and when quite boiling pour quickly into the basin, stirring thoroughly; stir occasionally until quite cold, then pour into custard glasses and grate a little nutmeg on the top, or put in a glass dish and serve with stewed or tinned fruits, or the custard can be used with Christmas or plum pudding instead of sauce.

When the custard has been standing over night, it should be well stirred before using.

CUSTARD IN PASTRY OR KENTISH PUDDING PIE.

Line a pie-dish with puff paste, prick well with a fork and bake carefully, then fill the case with a custard made as follows. Mix 1 dessertspoonful of flour with the contents of a packet of Allinson custard powder, out of a pint of milk take 8 tablespoonfuls and mix well with the flour, custard powder, &c., boil the remainder of milk with sugar to taste and 1 oz. of butter and when quite boiling pour on to the custard powder, stir quickly for a minute, then pour into the pastry case, grate a little nutmeg on the top and bake till of a golden brown; serve either hot or cold.

FRUMENTY.

1 quart of milk, 1/2 pint of ready boiled wheat (boiled in water), 1/4 lb. of sultanas and currants mixed, sugar to taste, 4 eggs, a stick of cinnamon. Mix the milk with the wheat (which should be fresh), the sugar and fruit, adding the cinnamon, and let all cook gently over a low fire, stirring frequently; when the mixture is nicely thickened remove it from the fire and let it cool; beat up the eggs and gradually mix them with the rest, taking great care not to curdle them. Stir the frumenty over the fire, but do not allow to boil. Serve hot or cold. The wheat should be fresh and soaked for 24 hours, and then cooked from 3 to 5 hours.

GOOSEBERRY CUSTARD.

Make some good puff paste and line a pie-dish with it, putting a double row round the edge. With 1/2 lb. of castor sugar stew 1 lb. of green gooseberries until the skins are tender, then rub them through a sieve. Scald 1 pint of milk, mix 1 tablespoonful of Allinson cornflour to a smooth paste with cold milk, add it to the milk when boiling, let it boil for 5 minutes, gently stirring it all the time, then turn it into a bowl and let it become cool. Add 1/4 lb. of castor sugar, 2 oz. of butter melted and dropped in gradually whilst the mixture is beaten, then put in the well-beaten yolks of 6 eggs, add the mashed gooseberries in small quantities, and lastly the whites of the eggs whipped to a stiff froth; beat all together for a minute to mix well. Pour this into the lined pie-dish and bake 25 or 30 minutes; serve in the pie-dish. This can be made from any kind of acid fruit, and is as good cold as hot.

GOOSEBERRY FOOL.

Top and tail 1 pint of gooseberries, put into a lined saucepan with sugar to taste and half a small teacupful of water, stew gently until perfectly tender, rub through a sieve, and when quite cold add 1 pint of custard made with Allinson custard powder, which should have been allowed to become cold before being mixed with the fruit. Serve in a glass dish with sponge fingers.

N.B.—Apple fool is made in exactly the same way as above, substituting sharp apples for the gooseberries.

MACARONI CUSTARD.

4 oz. of Allinson macaroni, 3 eggs, 1 tablespoonful of sugar, 1 even dessertspoonful of Allinson cornflour, vanilla to taste. Boil the macaroni in 1 pint of milk, and add a little water it needed; when quite tender place it on a glass dish to cool; make a custard of the rest of the milk and the other ingredients; flavour it well with vanilla; when the custard is cool pour it over the macaroni, and serve with or without stewed fruit.

MACAROON CUSTARD.

1/2 lb. of macaroons, 1 quart of milk, 6 eggs, 1 dessertspoonful of Allinson cornflour, sugar and vanilla essence to taste. Boil the milk and stir into it the cornflour smoothed with a little of the milk; whip up the eggs, and carefully stir in the milk (which should have been allowed to go off the boil) without curdling it; add sugar and vanilla to taste, and stir the custard over the fire until it thickens, placing it in a jug into a saucepan of boiling water. Arrange the macaroons in a glass dish, and when the custard is cool enough not to crack the dish, pour it over them and sprinkle some ground almonds on the top. Serve cold.

ORANGE CUSTARD.

The juice of 6 oranges and of 1/2 a lemon, 6 eggs, 6 oz. of sugar, and 1 dessertspoonful of Allinson cornflour. Add enough water to the fruit juices to make 1-1/2 pints of liquid. Set this over the fire with the sugar; meanwhile smooth the cornflour with a little cold water, and thicken the liquid with it when boiling. Set aside the saucepan, (which should be an enamelled one) so as to cool the contents a little. Beat up the eggs, gradually stir into them the thickened liquid, and then proceed with the custard as in the previous recipe. This is a German sweet, and very delicious.

RASPBERRY CUSTARD.

1-1/2 pints of raspberries, 1/2 pint of red currants, 6 oz. of sugar, 7 eggs, 1 dessertspoonful of Allinson cornflour. Mix the fruit, and let it cook from 5 to 10 minutes with 1 pint of water; strain the juice well through a piece of muslin or a fine hair-sieve. There should be 1 quart of juice; if necessary add a little more water; return the juice to the saucepan, add the sugar and reheat the liquid; when it boils thicken it with the cornflour, then set it aside to cool. Beat up the eggs, add them carefully after the fruit juice has somewhat cooled; stir the custard over the fire until it thickens, but do not allow it to boil, as the eggs would curdle. Serve cold in custard glasses, or in a glass dish poured over macaroons or sponge cakes. You can make a fruit custard in this way, with strawberries, cherries, red currants, or any juicy summer fruit.

STRAWBERRY CUSTARD.

Remove the stalks from 1 lb. of fresh strawberries, place them in a glass dish and scatter over 2 tablespoonfuls of pounded sugar; prepare 1 pint of custard with Allinson custard powder according to recipe given above, and while still hot pour carefully over the fruit, set aside to cool, and just before serving (which must not be until the custard has become quite cold) garnish the top with a few fine strawberries.

APPLE COOKERY

APPLES (BUTTERED).

1 lb. of apples, 2 oz. of butter, ground cinnamon and sugar to taste. Pare, core, and slice the apples; heat the butter in a frying-pan, when it boils turn in the apples and fry them until cooked; sprinkle with sugar and cinnamon, and serve on buttered toast.

APPLE CAKE

6 oz. each of Allinson fine wheatmeal and white flour, 4-1/2 oz. of butter, 1 egg, a little cold water, 1-1/2 lbs. of apples, 1 heaped-up teaspoonful of cinnamon, and 3 oz. of castor sugar. Rub the butter into the meal and flour, beat up the egg and add it, and as much cold water as is required to make a smooth paste; roll out the greater part of it 1/4 inch thick, and line a flat buttered tin with it. Pare, core, and cut the apples into thin divisions, arrange them in close rows on the paste point down, leaving 1 inch of edge uncovered; sift the sugar and cinnamon over the apples; roll out thinly the rest of the paste, cover the apples with it, turn up the edges of the bottom crust over the edges of the top crust, make 2 incisions in the crust, and bake the cake until brown in a moderately hot oven; when cold sift castor sugar over it, slip the cake off the tin, cut into pieces, and serve.

APPLE CHARLOTTE.

2 lbs. of good cooking apples, 2 oz. of chopped almonds, 4 oz. of currants and sultanas mixed, 1 stick of cinnamon about 3 inches long, sugar to taste,

the juice of 1/2 a lemon, and Allinson bread and butter cut very thinly. Pare, core, and cut up the apples, and stew them with a teacupful of water and the cinnamon, until the apples have become a pulp; remove the cinnamon, and add sugar, lemon juice, the almonds, and the currants and sultanas, previously picked, washed, and dried; mix all well and allow the mixture to cool; butter a pie-dish and line it with thin slices of bread and butter, then place on it a layer of apple mixture, repeat the layers, finishing with slices of bread and butter; bake for 3/4 hour in a moderate oven.

APPLES (DRYING).

Those who have apple-trees are often at a loss to know what to do with the windfalls. The apples come down on some days by the bushel, and it is impossible to use them all up for apple pie, puddings, or jelly. An excellent way to keep them for winter use is to dry them. It gives a little trouble, but one is well repaid for it, for the home-dried apples are superior in flavour to any bought apple-rings or pippins. Peel your apples, cut away the cores and all the worm-eaten parts—for nearly the whole of the windfalls are more or less worm-eaten. The good parts cut into thin pieces, spread them on large sheets of paper in the sun. In the evening (before the dew falls), they should be taken indoors and spread on tins (but with paper underneath), on the cool kitchen stove, and if the oven is only just warm, placed in the oven well spread out; of course they require frequent turning about, both in the sun and on the stove. Next day they may again be spread in the sun, and will probably be quite dry in the course of the day. Should the weather be rainy, the apples must be dried indoors only, and extra care must then be taken that they are neither scorched nor cooked on the stove. Whilst cooking is going on they will dry nicely on sheets of paper on the plate-rack. When the apples are quite dry, which is when the outside is not moist at all, fill them into brown paper bags and hang them up in an airy, dry place. The apples will be found delicious in flavour when stewed, and most acceptable when fresh fruit is scarce. I have dried several bushels of apples in this way every year.

APPLE DUMPLINGS.

Core as many apples as may be required. Fill the holes with a mixture of sugar and cinnamon; make a paste for a short crust, roll it out, and wrap each apple in it. Bake the dumplings about 30 or 40 minutes in the oven, or boil them the same time in plenty of water, placing the dumplings in the water when it boils fast. Serve with cream or sweet white sauce.

APPLE FOOL.

2 lbs. of apples, 1/2 lb. of dates, 3/4 pint of milk, 1/4 pint of cream, 6 cloves tied in muslin, and a little sugar. Pare, core, and cut up the apples, stone the dates, and gently stew the fruit with a teacupful of water and the cloves until quite tender; when sufficiently cooked, remove the cloves, and rub the fruit through a sieve; gradually mix in the milk, which should be boiling, then the cream; serve cold with sponge-cake fingers.

APPLE FRITTERS.

3 good juicy cooking apples, 3 eggs, 6 oz. of Allinson fine wheatmeal, 1/2 pint of milk, and sugar to taste. Pare and core the apples, and cut them into rounds 1/4 inch thick; make a batter with the milk, meal, and the eggs well beaten, adding sugar to taste. Have a frying-pan ready on the fire with boiling oil, vege-butter, or butter, dip the apple slices into the batter and fry the fritters until golden brown; drain them on blotting paper, and keep them hot in the oven until all are done.

APPLE JELLY.

1 pint of water to each 1 lb. of apples. Wash and cut up the apples, and boil them in the water until tender; then pour them into a jelly bag and let drain

well; take 1 lb. of loaf sugar to each pint of juice, and the juice of 1 lemon to each quart of liquid. Boil the liquid, skimming carefully, until the jelly sets when cold if a drop is tried on a plate. It may take from 2 hours to 3 hours in boiling.

APPLE PANCAKES.

Make the batter as directed in the recipe for "Apple Fritters," peel 2 apples, and cut them in thin slices, mix them with the batter, add sugar and cinnamon to taste, a little lemon juice if liked, and fry the pancakes in the usual way.

APPLE PUDDING.

1-1/2 lbs. of apples, 1 teaspoonful of ground cinnamon, sugar to taste, 1/2 lb. of Allinson fine wheatmeal, and 2-1/2 oz. of butter or vege-butter. Pare, core, and cut up the apples; make a paste of the meal, butter and a little cold water; roll the paste out, line a pudding basin with the greater part of it, put in the apples, and sprinkle over them the cinnamon and 4 oz. of sugar—a little more should the apples be very sour; cover the apples with the rest of the paste, and press the edges together round the sides; tie a cloth over the basin and boil the pudding for 2-1/2 to 3 hours in a saucepan with boiling water.

APPLE PUDDING (Nottingham).

6 baking apples, 2 oz. of sugar, 1 heaped up teaspoonful of ground cinnamon, 3/4 pint of milk, 3 eggs, 6 oz. of Allinson wholemeal, and 1 oz. of butter. Core the apples, mix the sugar and cinnamon, and fill the hole where the core was with it; put the apples into a buttered pie-dish; make a batter of the milk, eggs, and meal, melt the butter and mix it into the batter;

pour it over the apples, and bake the pudding for 2 hours in a moderate oven.

APPLE SAGO.

5 oz. of sago, 1-1/2 lbs. of apples, the juice of a lemon, a teaspoonful of ground cinnamon, and sugar to taste. Wash the sago and cook it in 1-1/2 pints of water, to which the cinnamon is added; meanwhile have the apples ready, pared, cored, and cut up; cook them in very little water, just enough to keep the apples from burning; when they are quite soft rub them through a sieve and mix them with the cooking sago, adding sugar and lemon juice; let all cook gently for a few minutes or until the sago is quite soft; put the mixture into a wetted mould, and turn out when cold.

APPLE SAUCE.

1 lb. of good cooking apples, sugar to taste. Pare, core, and cut in pieces the apples, cook them in a few spoonfuls of water to prevent them burning; when quite soft rub the apple through a sieve, and sweeten the sauce to taste. Rubbing the sauce through a sieve ensures the sauce being free from pieces should the apple not pulp evenly.

APPLE TART (OPEN).

2 lbs. of apples, 1 cupful of currants and sultanas, 2 oz. of chopped almonds, sugar to taste, 1 teaspoonful of ground cinnamon or the rind of 1/2 lemon (which latter should be removed after cooking with the apples), 12 oz. or Allinson fine wheatmeal, and 4-1/2 oz. of butter. Pare, core, and cut up the apples; stew them in very little water, only just enough to keep from burning; when nearly done add the currants, sultanas, almonds, cinnamon, and sugar; let all simmer together until the apples have become a pulp; let

the fruit cool; make a paste of the meal, butter, and a little water; roll it out and line a round, flat dish with it, and brush the paste over with white of eggs; turn the apple mixture on the paste; cut the rest of the paste into strips 3/8 of an inch wide, and lay them over the apples in diamond shape, each 1 inch from the other, so as to make a kind of trellis arrangement of the pastry. If enough paste is left, lay a thin strip right round the dish to finish off the edge, mark it nicely with a fork or spoon, and bake the tart for 3/4 hour. Serve with white sauce or custard.

APPLES (RICE)

2 lbs. of apples, 1/2 lb. of rice, the rind of 1/2 lemon (or a piece of stick cinnamon if preferred), 4 oz. of sultanas, sugar to taste, 1 oz. of butter, and, if the apples are not sour, the juice of a lemon. Boil the rice in 3 pints of water with the lemon rind, then add the apples, pared, cored, and sliced, the sultanas, butter, lemon juice, and sugar; let all simmer gently for 1/2 hour, or until quite tender; if too dry add a little more water; remove the lemon rind before serving.

EVE PUDDING.

1/2 lb. each of apples and breadcrumbs, and 1/2 lb. of currants and sultanas mixed, 5 eggs well beaten, sugar to taste, the grated rind and juice of 1 lemon, and 2 oz. of butter. Peel, core, and chop small the apples, mix them with the breadcrumbs, sugar, currants, and sultanas (washed and picked), the lemon juice and rind, and the butter, previously melted; whip up the eggs and mix them well with the other ingredients; turn the mixture into a buttered mould, tie with a cloth, and steam the pudding for 3 hours.

BREAD AND CAKES

THE ADVANTAGES OF WHOLEMEAL BREAD.

People are now concerning themselves about the foods they eat, and inquiring into their properties, composition, and suitability. One food that is now receiving a good deal of attention is bread, and we ought to be sure that this is of the best kind, for as a nation we eat daily a pound of it per head. We consume more of this article of food than of any other, and this is as it ought to be, for bread is the staff of life, and many of the other things we eat are garnishings. It is said we cannot live on bread alone, but this is untrue if the loaf is a proper one; at one time our prisoners were fed on it alone, and the peasantry of many countries live on very little else.

Not many years ago books treating of food and nutrition always gave milk as the standard food, and so it is for calves and babies. Nowadays we use a grain food as the standard, and of all grains wheat is the one which is nearest perfection, or which supplies to the body those elements that it requires, and in best proportions. A perfect food must contain carbonaceous, nitrogenous, and mineral matter in definite quantities; there must be from four to six parts of carbonaceous or heat and force-forming matter to one of nitrogen, and from two to four per cent. of mineral matter; also a certain bulk of innutritious matter for exciting secretion, for separating the particles of food so that the various gastric and intestinal juices may penetrate and dissolve out all the nutriment, and for carrying off the excess of the biliary and other intestinal secretions with the fæces.

A grain of wheat consists of an outer hard covering or skin, a layer of nitrogenous matter directly under this, and an inner kernel of almost pure starch. The average composition of wheat is this:—

```
              Nitrogen          12
              Carbon            72
              Mineral Matter     4
              Water             12
```

From this analysis we observe that the nitrogenous matter is to the carbonaceous in the proportion of one-sixth, which is the composition of a perfect food. Besides taking part in this composition, the bran, being in a great measure insoluble, passes in bulk through the bowels, assisting daily laxation—a most important consideration. If wheat is such a perfect food, it must follow that wholemeal bread must be best for our daily use. That such is the case, evidence on every side shows; those who eat it are healthier, stronger, and more cheerful than those who do not, all other things being equal. Wholemeal bread comes nearer the standard of a perfect food than does the wheaten grain, as in fermentation some of the starch is destroyed, and thus the proportion of nitrogen is slightly increased.

The next question is, how shall we prepare the grain so as to make the best bread from it? This is done by grinding the grain as finely as possible with stones, and then using the resulting flour for bread-making. The grain should be first cleaned and brushed, and passed over a magnet to cleanse it from any bits of steel or iron it may have acquired from the various processes it goes through, and then finely ground. To ensure fine grinding, it is always advisable to kiln-dry it first. When ground, nothing must be taken from it, nor must anything be added to the flour, and from this bread should be made. Baking powder, soda, and tartaric acid, or soda and hydrochloric acid, or ammonia and hydrochloric acid, or other chemical agents, must never be used for raising bread, as these substances are injurious, and affect the human system for harm. The only ferment that should be used is yeast; of this the French variety is best. If brewer's yeast is used it must be first well washed, otherwise it gives a bitter flavour to the loaf. A small quantity of salt may be used, but not much, otherwise it adds an injurious agent to the bread.

BARLEY BANNOCKS.

Put 1/2 pint of milk into a saucepan allow it to boil; then sprinkle in barley meal, stirring it constantly to prevent lumps till the mixture is quite thick and almost unstirrable. Turn the mass out on a meal-besprinkled board and leave to cool. When cool enough to knead, work it quite stiff with dry meal, take a portion off, roll it as thin as a wafer, and bake it on a hot girdle; when done on one side, turn and cook on the other. The girdle is to be swept clean after each bannock. Eat hot or cold with butter.

BUN LOAF.

1 lb. Allinson wholemeal flour, 1/2 lb. butter, 1/2 lb. brown sugar, 1/4 lb. currants, 1/4 lb. raisins, 1/4 lb. candied peel, 4 eggs, 1/2 teacupful of milk. Mix the flour, sugar, currants, raisins, candied peel (cut in thin strips), the butter and eggs well together; mix with the milk; pour into a buttered tin, and bake in a moderate oven for 2 hours.

BUNS (1).

1 lb. flour, 1/4 lb. sugar, 4 oz. currants, 2 oz. butter, or vege-butter, 1 teacupful of milk, 1 oz. French yeast, 2 eggs, a little salt. Mix the flour, sugar, salt, and currants in a basin, warm the butter and milk slightly, mix it smoothly with the yeast, then add the eggs well beaten; pour this on the flour, stirring well together till it is all moistened; when thoroughly mixed, set it to rise by the fire for 1/2 hour; make into buns, set to rise by the fire for 10 minutes, brush the tops over with egg, and bake from 10 to 15 minutes.

BUNS (2).

1/2 pint water, 1/2 pint milk, 1 oz. yeast, 1 oz. sugar, 6 oz. Allinson's wholemeal, 1 egg (not necessary). Warm water and milk to 105 degrees, dissolve sugar and yeast in it and stir in the meal, leave well covered up in a warm place for 45 minutes. Then have ready 1 3/4 lbs. Allinson's wholemeal, 1/4 lb. vege-butter, 5 oz. sugar, 1/2 lb. currants, pinch of salt. Melt down vege-butter to oil, make bay of meal, sprinkle currants round, stir the sugar and salt with the ferment till dissolved, then mix in the melted butter and make up into a dough with the meal and currants. Keep in warm place for 45 minutes, then knock gas out of dough and leave 1/2 hour more; shape buns, place on warm greased tin, prove 15 minutes and bake in moderately warm oven for 20 minutes.

BUNS (PLAIN).

1 lb. flour, 6 oz. butter, or vege-butter, 1/4 lb. sugar, 1 egg, 1/4 pint milk, 15 drops essence of lemon. Warm the butter without oiling it, beat it with a wooden spoon, stir the flour in gradually with the sugar, and mix the ingredients well together; make the milk lukewarm, beat up with it the egg and lemon and stir to the flour; beat the dough well for 10 minutes, divide into 24 pieces, put into patty pans, and bake in a brisk oven for from 20 to 30 minutes.

BUTTER BISCUITS.

1/2 lb. butter, 2 lbs. fine wholemeal flour, 1/2 pint milk. Dissolve the butter in the milk, which should be warmed, then stir in the meal and make into a stiff, smooth paste, roll it out very thin, stamp it into biscuits, prick them out with a fork, and bake on tins in a quick oven for 10 minutes.

BUTTERMILK CAKE.

2 lbs. Allinson wholemeal flour, 2 lbs. currants, 1/2 lb. sugar, 12 oz. butter, 2 oz. candied lemon peel, 1 pint buttermilk. Beat the butter to a cream, add

the sugar, then the meal, fruit, and milk, mix thoroughly; butter a cake tin, pour in the mixture, and bake in a slow oven for 3 1/2 hours.

BUTTERMILK CAKES.

2 lbs. wholemeal flour, 1 pint buttermilk, 1 teaspoonful salt. Mix the meal well with the salt, add the buttermilk and pour on the flour; beat well together, roll it out, cut into cakes, and bake for from 15 to 20 minutes in a quick oven.

CHOCOLATE BISCUITS.

2 oz. of powdered chocolate, 2 oz. of white sugar, 2 whites of eggs beaten to a stiff froth. Mix all together, and drop in biscuits on white or wafer paper. Bake 16 minutes in a moderate oven.

CHOCOLATE CAKE (1).

1/2 lb. of fine wheatmeal, 1/4 lb. of butter, 5 eggs, 1/2 lb. of castor sugar, 1-1/2 oz. of Allinson cocoa, 1 dessertspoonful of vanilla essence. Proceed as in recipe of "Madeira Cake," adding the cocoa and flavouring with vanilla.

CHOCOLATE CAKE (2).

Work 4 oz. of butter to a cream, add a 1/4 lb. of castor sugar, 3 eggs, and a little milk. Mix together 1/2 lb. of Allinson fine wheatmeal, a heaped tablespoonful of cocoa. Add to the butter mixture, and bake on a shallow tin or plate in a quick oven. The cake can be iced when done, and cut, when cold, into diamond-shaped pieces or triangles.

CHOCOLATE MACAROONS.

1/2 lb. of ground sweet almonds, 1 oz. of cocoa, 1 dessertspoonful of vanilla essence, 1/2 lb. of castor sugar, the white of 4 eggs. Whip the white of the eggs to a stiff froth, add the sugar, cocoa, vanilla, and almond meal, and proceed as in the previous recipe.

CINNAMON MADEIRA CAKE.

1/2 lb. of fine wheatmeal, 1/4 lb. of butter, 1/2 lb. of sugar, 1/4 lb. of currants and sultanas mixed (washed and picked) 5 eggs, 1 dessertspoonful of ground cinnamon. Proceed as in recipe for "Madeira Cake," adding the fruit, and cinnamon as flavouring.

COCOANUT BISCUITS.

2 breakfastcupfuls of wheatmeal, 2 teacupfuls of grated cocoanut, 3 dessertspoonfuls of sugar, 3 tablespoonfuls of orange water, 2 oz. of butter, a little milk. Mix the ingredients, adding a little milk to moisten the paste, mix it well, roll the paste out 1/4 in. thick, cut out with a biscuit cutter. Prick the biscuits, and bake them in a moderate oven a pale brown.

COCOANUT DROPS.

1/2 lb. of desiccated cocoanut, 1/2 lb. of castor sugar, the whites of 3 eggs. Beat the whites of the eggs to a stiff froth, add the sugar, then the cocoanut. Place little lumps of the mixture on the rice wafer paper, as in recipe for "Macaroons," and bake in a fairly hot oven.

COCOANUT ROCK CAKES.

1 lb. of fine wholemeal flour, 6 oz. of desiccated cocoanut, 3 oz. of butter, 3 eggs, a little cold milk, 6 oz. castor sugar. Rub the butter into the meal, add the sugar, cocoanut, and the well-beaten eggs. Mix, and add only just enough milk to make the mixture keep together. Put small lumps on a floured baking tin, and bake in a quick oven.

CORNFLOUR CAKE.

1/2 lb. of cornflour, 4 eggs, 6 oz. butter, same of castor sugar; separate the yolks of eggs from the whites and beat separately for a 1/4 of an hour, cream the butter and sugar, mix with the yolks, then the whites, and lastly the flour, and whisk all together for 25 minutes, and bake for 1 hour in a moderately hot oven.

CRACKERS.

1 cupful butter, 1 teaspoonful salt, 2 quarts Allinson wholemeal flour. Rub thoroughly together with the hand, and wet up with cold water; beat well, and beat in meal to make brittle and hard; then pinch off pieces and roll out each cracker by itself, if you wish them to resemble baker's crackers.

CRISP OATMEAL CAKES.

1 lb. of oatmeal, 2 oz. of butter or oil (1 tablespoonful of oil is 1 oz.), 1 gill of cold milk. Make a dough of the butter, meal, and milk; shake meal plentifully on the board, turn the dough on to it, and having sprinkled this too with meal, work it a little with the backs of your fingers. Roll the dough

out to the thickness of a crown piece, cut it in shapes, put the cakes on a hot stove, and when they are a little brown on the underside, take them off and place them on a hanger in front of the fire in order to brown the upper side; when this is done they are ready for use.

DYSPEPTICS' BREAD.

9 oz. of Allinson wholemeal, 1 egg, a scant 1/2 pint of milk and water. Separate the yolk from the white of the egg. Beat up the yolk with the milk and water, and mix this with the meal into a thick batter; whip up the white of the egg stiff, and mix it well into the batter. Grease and heat a bread tin, turn the mixture into it, and bake the loaf for 1-1/2 hours in a hot oven. This is very delicious bread, very light and digestible.

DOUGHNUTS.

1-1/2 lbs. of wheatmeal, 1/4 oz. yeast, 1 egg, 1 teaspoonful of cinnamon, 3 tablespoonfuls of sugar, enough lukewarm milk to moisten the dough, some jam and marmalade. Dissolve the yeast in a little warm milk, mix all the ingredients, adding the dissolved yeast and enough milk to make the dough sufficiently moist to handle. Let it rise 1-1/2 hours in front of the stove. When risen roll it out 1/2 in. thick, cut out round pieces, place a little jam or marmalade in the middle, close up the dough, forming the dough nuts, and cook them in boiling oil or vege-butter until brown and thoroughly done. Eat warm.

GINGER SPONGE CAKE (a nice Cake for Children who do not like Gingerbread).

3 breakfast cups of Allinson wholemeal flour, 1 breakfast cup of sugar, 3 eggs, 6 oz. of butter or vege-butter, 2 heaped teaspoonfuls of ground ginger,

1 saltspoonful of salt, 1/2 gill milk. Beat the butter, sugar, and eggs to a cream, mix all the dry ingredients together; add gradually to the butter, &c., lastly the milk. Put into a well-greased tin, bake about 20 minutes in a quick oven. When cold cut into finger lengths or squares.

ICING FOR CAKES.

To 8 oz. of sugar take 2 whites of eggs, well beaten, and 1 tablespoonful of orange-or rosewater. Whisk the ingredients thoroughly, and when the cake is cold cover it with the mixture. Set the cake in the oven to harden, but do not let it remain long enough to discolour.

JUMBLES.

1 lb. of wheatmeal, 1 lb. of castor sugar, 1/2 pint of milk, 1/4 lb. of butter, 1 lb. ground almonds. Cream the butter, add the other ingredients, and moisten with a little rosewater. Roll out and cut the jumbles into any shape desired. Bake in a gentle oven.

LEMON CAKES.

1/2 lb. of castor sugar, 1/2 lb. of wheatmeal, sifted fine, the grated rind of a lemon, 2 oz. of butter, and 2 well-beaten eggs. Rub the butter into the meal, and mix all the ingredients well together; roll the mixture out thin, lay it on a tin, and when baked cut into diamond squares.

LIGHT CAKE.

2 lbs. of brown breadcrumbs, 1/2 lb. of sultanas, 3 eggs, yolks and whites beaten separately; 2 oz. of butter, as much milk as required to moisten 1/4 lb. of sugar. Rub the butter into the breadcrumbs, add the fruit, sugar, yolks, and lukewarm milk. At the last add the whites beaten to a stiff froth. Put the mixture in a well-greased tin, and bake 1 hour in a moderate oven.

LUNCH CAKE.

A good lunch cake may be made by rubbing 6 oz. of butter into 1-1/4 lbs. of Allinson wholemeal flour, 6 oz. of sugar. Beat up the yolks of 4 eggs with a teacupful of milk, and work into the flour so as to make a stiff batter. Add 2 oz. of mixed peel cut small, and 1/2 lb. of mixed sultanas. Lastly, add the beaten white of the eggs, whisk well, and pour the mixture into a greased cake tin. Bake for 1-1/2 to 2 hours.

MACAROON.

1/2 lb. of ground sweet almonds, 1 oz. of ground bitter almonds, a few sliced almonds, the whites of 4 eggs, and 1/2 lb. of castor sugar. Whip the whites of the eggs to a stiff froth, add the sugar, then the almond meal, and mix all well; if the mixture seems very stiff add one or two teaspoonfuls of water. Lay sheets of kitchen paper on tins, over this sheets of rice wafers (or, as it is also called, "wafer paper"), which can be obtained from confectioners and large stores; drop little lumps of the mixture on the wafers, allowing room for the spreading of the macaroons, place a couple of pieces of sliced almond on each, and bake them in a quick oven until they are set and don't feel wet to the touch. If the macaroons brown too much, place a sheet of paper lightly over them.

MADEIRA CAKE.

1/2 lb. of fine wheatmeal, 1/2 lb. of castor sugar, 1/2 lb. of butter, 5 eggs, flavouring to taste. Beat the butter to a cream, add the sugar, then the eggs well beaten, the meal and the flavouring. Line a cake tin with buttered paper, and bake the cake in a moderate oven from 1 to 1-1/2 hours.

OATMEAL BANNOCKS.

Cold porridge, Allinson fine wheatmeal. Stir sufficient of the meal into any cold porridge that may be left over to form a dough just firm enough to roll out. Well grease and sprinkle with flour some baking sheets, roll the dough to the thickness of 1/2 an inch, cut into triangular shapes, and bake until brown on both sides. Butter and serve hot.

OATMEAL FINGER-ROLLS.

Use equal parts of medium oatmeal and Allinson fine wheatmeal, and add a good 1/2 pint of milk and water to 1 pound of the mixed meal. Knead into a dough, make it into finger-rolls about 3 inches long, and bake them in a quick oven from 30 to 40 minutes.

ORANGE CAKES.

6 oz. of Allinson wholemeal flour, 3 oz. butter, 4 oz. sugar, grate in the rind of 1 small orange, and mix all well together. Beat 1 egg, and stir in with the juice of the orange and sufficient buttermilk to make a smooth, thick batter. Half fill small greased tins with this mixture, and bake 15 minutes in a moderate oven.

MISCELLANEOUS

A DISH OF SNOW.

1 pint of thick apple sauce, sweetened and flavoured to taste (orange or rosewater is preferable), the whites of 3 eggs, beaten to a stiff froth. Mix both together, and serve.

CAULIFLOWER AU GRATIN.

A fair-sized cauliflower, 1 pint of milk, 1-1/2 oz. of dried Allinson breadcrumbs, 3 oz. of cheese, 1-1/2 oz. of butter, 1 heaped-up tablespoonful of Allinson wholemeal flour, a little nutmeg, and pepper and salt to taste. Boil the cauliflower until half cooked, cut it into pieces, and place them in a pie-dish. Boil the milk, adding the seasoning, 1/2 oz. of the butter, and 1/2 a saltspoonful of the nutmeg. Thicken with the wholemeal smoothed in a little cold milk or water. Stir in the cheese and pour the sauce over the cauliflower. Shake the breadcrumbs over the top, cut the rest of the butter in bits, and place them over the breadcrumbs. Bake for 20 minutes to 1/2 an hour, or until the cauliflower is soft.

COMPÔTE OF ORANGES AND APPLES.

6 oranges, 8 fine sweet apples, 1 oz. of ground sweet almonds, syrup as in "Orange Syrup." Peel the oranges and the apples, cut them across in thin slices, coring the apples and removing the pips from the oranges. Arrange the fruit into alternate circles in a glass dish, sprinkling the ground almonds between the layers. Pour over the whole the syrup. Serve when cold.

CRUST FOR MINCE PIES.

1/2 lb. of Allinson fine wheatmeal, 1/2 lb. of medium oatmeal, 6 oz. of butter or vege-butter, 1 cupful of cold water. Rub the butter into the flour, add the water, and mix all into a paste with a knife. Roll the paste out thin on a floured board, cut pieces out with a tumbler or biscuit cutter. Line with them small patty pans, and fill them with mincemeat; cover with paste, moisten the edges and press them together, and bake the mince pies in a quick oven; they will be done in 15 to 20 minutes.

GROUND RICE PANCAKES.

4 oz. of ground rice, 4 eggs, 1 pint of milk, jam, some sifted sugar, and powdered cinnamon; butter or oil for frying. Make a batter of the milk, eggs, and ground rice. Fry thin pancakes of the mixture, sprinkle them with sugar and cinnamon, place a dessertspoonful of jam on each, fold up, sprinkle with a little more sugar; keep hot until all the pancakes are fried, and serve them very hot. When the pancakes are golden brown on one side, they should be slipped on a plate, turned back into the frying-pan, and fried brown on the other side.

MACARONI PANCAKES.

2 oz. of macaroni, 1/2 pint of milk, 3 eggs, 3 oz. of Allinson fine wheatmeal, sugar to taste, the grated rind of a lemon, butter, and 1 whole lemon. Throw the macaroni into boiling water and boil until quite soft; drain it and cut it into pieces 1 inch long. Make a batter of the eggs, meal, and milk, add the lemon rind, sugar, and the macaroni; fry pancakes of the mixture, using a small piece of butter not bigger than a walnut for each pancake. Sift sugar over the pancakes and serve them very hot with slices of lemon.

MINCEMEAT.

1 lb. of apples, 1 lb. of stoned raisins, 1 lb. of currants, 6 oz. of citron peel, 3 oz. of blanched almonds, 1/2 lb. butter. Chop the fruit up very finely, add the almonds cut up fine, oil the butter and mix well with the fruit. Turn the mincemeat into little jars, cover tightly, and keep in a dry and cool place.

MINCEMEAT (another).

1 lb. each of raisins, apples, and currants, 1/2 lb. of butter, 1/2 lb. of blanched and chopped almonds, 1/2 lb. of moist sugar, the juice of 4 lemons, and 1/2 lb. of mixed peel. Wash and pick the currants, wash and stone the raisins, peel, core, and quarter the apples, and cut up the mixed peel; then mince all up together, and add the chopped almonds. Melt the butter, mix it thoroughly with the fruit, fill it into one or more jars, cover with paper, and tie down tightly.

ORANGE FLOWER PUFF.

1/2 pint of milk, 3 eggs, 4 ozs. of Allinson fine wheatmeal, and 2 tablespoonfuls of orange water, some butter or oil for frying. Make a batter of the milk, eggs (well beaten), and meal, add the orange water, and fry the batter in thin pancakes, powder with castor sugar, and serve.

ORANGE SYRUP.

The rind of 3 oranges, 1/2 pint of water, 4 oz. of sugar. Boil the ingredients until the syrup is clear, then strain it and pour over the fruit.

ORANGES IN SYRUP.

Peel 6 oranges, carefully removing all the white pith. Put the rinds of these into 1/2 pint of cold water; boil it gently for 10 minutes. Strain, and add to the water 6 oz, of loaf sugar. Boil it until it is a thick syrup, then drop into it the oranges, divided in sections, without breaking the skins. Only a few minutes cooking will be needed. The oranges are nicest served cold.

RASPBERRY FROTH.

The whites of 5 eggs, 3 tablespoonfuls of raspberry jam. Beat the whites of the eggs to a very stiff froth, then beat the jam up with it and serve at once in custard glasses. This recipe can be varied by using various kinds of jam.

RICE FRITTERS.

6 oz. of rice, 1 pint of milk, 8 oz. of sugar, 1 oz. of fresh butter, 6 oz. of apricot marmalade, 3 eggs. Let the rice swell in the milk with the butter and the sugar over a slow fire until it is tender—this will take about 1/2 of an hour; when the rice is done, strain off any milk there may be left. Mix in the apricot marmalade and the beaten eggs, stir it well over the fire until the eggs are set; then spread the mixture on a dish, about 1/2 an inch thick. When it is quite cold, cut it in long strips, dip them in a batter, and fry them a nice brown. Strew sifted sugar over them, and serve.

SNOWBALLS.

1-1/2 pints of milk, 4 eggs, sugar and vanilla to taste, and 1 tablespoonful of cornflour. Boil the milk with sugar and a piece of vanilla or with 1 dessertspoonful of vanilla essence. Smooth the cornflour with a little cold milk, and thicken the milk with it. Whip the whites of the eggs to a very stiff froth with 1 spoonful of castor sugar, and drop spoonfuls of the froth into the boiling milk. Allow to boil until the balls are well set, turning them over that both sides may get done. Lift the balls out with a slice, and place them in a glass dish. Beat up the yolks of the eggs, stir them carefully in the hot milk; let the custard cool, and pour it into the glass dish, but not over the snowballs, which should remain white.

SPONGE MOULD.

9 stale sponge cakes, some raspberry jam, 2 pints of milk, 8 oz. of Allinson cornflour, sugar to taste, a few drops of almond essence. Halve the sponge cakes, spread them with jam, arrange them in a buttered mould, and soak them with 1/2 pint of the milk boiling hot. Boil the rest of the milk and thicken it with the cornflour as for blancmange; flavour with the essence and sugar; pour the mixture over the sponge cakes, and turn all out when cold.

STEWED PEARS AND VANILLA CREAM.

Get 1 tin of pears, open it, and turn the contents into an enamelled stewpan, add some sugar and liquid cochineal to colour the fruit, and let them stew a few minutes. Take out the pears carefully without breaking them, and let the syrup cook until it is thick. When the pears are cold lay them on a dish with the cores upwards, and with a spoon scoop out the core, and fill the space left with whipped cream flavoured with vanilla and sweetened; sprinkle them with finely shredded blanched almonds or pistachios, and pour the syrup round them.

SWISS CREAMS.

4 oz. of macaroons, a little raisin wine and 1 pint of custard, made with Allinson custard powder; lay the macaroons in a glass dish and pour over enough raisin wine to soak them, make the custard in the usual way, let it cool and then pour over the cakes; when quite cold garnish with pieces of bright coloured jelly.

TAPIOCA ICE.

1 teacupful of tapioca, 1/2 teacupful of sifted sugar, 1 tinned pineapple. Soak the tapioca over night in cold water; in the morning boil it in 1 quart of water until perfectly clear, and add the sugar and pineapple syrup. Chop up the pineapple and mix it with the boiling hot tapioca; turn the mixture into a wet mould. When cold turn it out and serve with cream and sugar.

TIPSY CAKE.

A WEEK'S MENU

I have written the following menus to help those who are beginning vegetarianism. When first starting, most housewives do not know what to provide, and this is a source of anxiety. I occasionally meet some who have been vegetarians a long time, but confess that they do not know how to provide a nice meal. They usually eat the plainest foods, because they know of no tasty dishes. When visitors come, we like to provide tempting dishes for them, and show them that appetising meals can be prepared without the carcases of animals. I only give seven menus, that is, one for each day of the week; but our dishes can be so varied that we can have a different menu daily for weeks without any repetition. The recipes here written give a fair idea to start with. Instead of always using butter beans, or haricot beans, as directed in one of these menus, lentils or split peas can be substituted. I have not included macaroni cheese in these menus, because this dish is so generally known; it can be introduced into any vegetarian dinner. I have allowed three courses at the dinner, but they are really not necessary. I give them to make the menus more complete. A substantial soup and a pudding, or a savoury with vegetables and sauce and a pudding, are sufficient for a good meal. In our own household we rarely have more than two courses, and often only one course. This article will be of assistance to all those who are wishing to try a healthful and humane diet, and to those meat eaters who wish to provide tasty meals for vegetarian friends.

Anna P. Allinson.

4, Spanish Place,
Manchester Square,
London, W.

MENU I.

TOMATO SOUP.

1 tin of tomatoes or 2 lbs. of fresh ones, 1 large Spanish onion or 1/2 lb. of smaller ones, 2 oz. of butter, pepper and salt to taste, 1 oz. of vermicelli and 2 bay leaves. Peel the onions and chop up roughly; brown them with the butter in the saucepan in which the soup is made. When the onion is browned, add the tomatoes (the fresh ones must be sliced) and 3 pints of water. Let all cook together for 1/2 an hour. Then drain the liquid through a sieve without rubbing anything through. Return the liquid to the saucepan, add the seasoning and the vermicelli; then allow the soup to cook until the vermicelli is soft, which will be in about 10 minutes. Sago, tapioca, or a little dried julienne may be used instead of the vermicelli.

VEGETABLE PIE.

1/2 lb. each of tomatoes, turnips, carrots, potatoes, 1 tablespoonful of sago, 1 teaspoonful of mixed herbs, 3 hard-boiled eggs, 2 oz. of butter, and pepper and salt to taste. Prepare the vegetables, scald and skin the tomatoes, cut them in pieces not bigger than a walnut, stew them in the butter and 1 pint of water until nearly tender, add the pepper and salt and the mixed herbs. When cooked, pour the vegetables into a pie-dish, sprinkle in the sago, add water to make gravy if necessary. Cut the hard-boiled eggs in quarters and place them on the top of the vegetables, cover with a crust made from Allinson wholemeal, and bake until it is brown.

SHORT CRUST.

10 oz. of Allinson wholemeal, 8 oz. of butter or vege-butter, 1 teacupful of cold water. Rub the butter into the meal, add the water, mixing the paste with a knife. Roll it out, cut strips to line the rim of the pie-dish, cover the vegetable with the crust, decorate it, and bake the pie as directed.

GOLDEN SYRUP PUDDING.

10 oz. of Allinson wholemeal, 3 eggs, 1 pint of milk, and 1/2 lb. of golden syrup. Grease a pudding basin, and pour the golden syrup into it; make a batter with the milk, meal, and eggs,

and pour this into the pudding basin on the syrup, but do not stir the batter up with the syrup. Place a piece of buttered paper on the top of the batter, tie a cloth over the basin unless you have a basin with a fitting metal lid, and steam the pudding for 2 1/2 hours in boiling water. Do not allow any water to boil into the pudding. Dip the basin with the pudding in it for 1 minute in cold water before turning it out, for then it comes out more easily.

MENU II.

CLEAR CELERY SOUP.

1 large head of celery or 2 small ones, 1 large Spanish onion, 2 oz. of butter, pepper and salt to taste, and 1 blade of mace. Chop the onion and fry it brown in the butter (or vege-butter) in the saucepan in which the soup is to be made. When brown, add 4 pints of water, the celery washed and cut into pieces, the mace, the pepper and salt. Let all cook until the celery is quite soft, then drain the liquid from the vegetables. Return it to the saucepan, boil the soup up, and add 1 oz. of vermicelli, sago, or Italian paste; let the soup cook until this is quite soft, and serve with sippets of Allinson wholemeal toast.

BUTTER BEANS WITH PARSLEY SAUCE.

Pick the beans, wash them and steep them over night in boiling water, just covering them. Allow 2 or 3 oz. of beans for each person. In the morning let them cook gently in the water they are steeped in, with the addition of a little butter, until quite soft, which will be in about 2 hours. The beans should be cooked in only enough water to keep them from burning; therefore, when it boils away, add only just sufficient for absorption. The sauce is made thus: 1 pint of milk, 1 tablespoonful of Allinson wholemeal, a handful of finely chopped parsley, the juice of 1/2 a lemon, pepper and salt to taste. Boil the milk and thicken it with the meal, which should first be smoothed with a little cold milk, then last of all add the lemon juice, the seasoning, and the parsley. This dish should be eaten with potatoes and green vegetables.

GROUND RICE PUDDING.

1 quart of milk, 6 oz. of ground rice, 1 egg, and any kind of jam. Boil the milk, stir into it the ground rice previously smoothed with some of the cold milk. Let the mixture gook gently for 5 minutes, stir frequently, draw the saucepan to the side, and when it has ceased to boil add the egg well whipped, and mix well. Pour half of the mixture into a pie-dish, spread a layer of jam over it, then pour the rest of the pudding mixture over the jam, and let it brown lightly in the oven.

MENU III.

CARROT SOUP.

4 good-sized carrots, 1 small head of celery, 1 fair sized onion, a turnip, 3 oz. of Allinson breadcrumbs, 1-1/2 oz. of butter, 1 blade of mace, pepper and salt to taste. Scrape and wash the vegetables, and cut them up small; set them over the fire with 3 pints of water, the butter, bread, and mace. Let all boil together until the vegetables are quite tender, and then rub them through a sieve. Return the mixture to the saucepan, season with pepper and salt, and if too thick add water to the soup, which should be as thick as cream. Boil the soup up, and serve.

CURRIED RICE AND TOMATOES.

1/2 lb. of Patna rice, 1 dessertspoonful of curry powder, salt to taste, and 1 oz. of butter. Wash the rice, put it over the fire in cold water, let it just boil up, then drain the water off. Mix 1 pint of cold water with the curry powder, put this over the fire with the rice, butter, and salt. Cover the rice with a piece of buttered paper and let it simmer gently until the water is absorbed. This will take about 20 minutes. Rice cooked this way will have all the grains separate. For the tomatoes proceed as follows: 1 lb. of tomatoes and a little butter, pepper, and salt. Wash the tomatoes and place them in a flat tin with a few spoonfuls of water; dust them with pepper and salt, and place little bits of butter on each tomato. Bake them from 15 to 20 minutes, according to the size of the tomatoes and the heat of the oven. Place the rice in the centre of a hot flat dish, put the tomatoes round it, pour the liquid over the rice, and serve.

APPLE CHARLOTTE.

2 lbs. of cooking apples, 1 teacupful of mixed currants and sultanas, 1 heaped-up teaspoonful of ground cinnamon, 2 oz. of blanched and chopped almonds, sugar to taste, Allinson wholemeal bread, and butter. Pare, core, and cut up the apples and set them to cook with a teacupful of water. Some apples require much more water than others. When they are soft add the fruit picked and washed, the cinnamon, and the almonds and sugar. Cut very thin slices of bread and butter, line a buttered pie-dish with them. Place a layer of apples over the buttered bread, and repeat the layers of bread and apples until the dish is full, finishing with a layer of bread and butter. Bake from 3/4 of an hour to 1 hour.

MENU IV.

RICE SOUP.

3 oz. of rice, 4 oz. of grated cheese, 1 breakfastcupful of tomato juice, 1 oz. of butter, pepper and salt to taste. Boil the rice till tender in 2-1/2 pints of water, with the butter and seasoning. When quite soft, add the tomato juice and the cheese; stir until the soup boils and the cheese is dissolved, and serve. If too much of the water has boiled away, add a little more.

HOT-POT.

2 lbs. of potatoes, 3/4 lb. of onions, 1 breakfastcupful of tinned tomatoes or 1/2 lb. of sliced fresh ones, 1 teaspoonful of mixed herbs, 1-1/2 oz. butter, pepper and salt to taste. Those who do not like tomatoes can leave them out, and the dish will still be very savoury. The potatoes should be peeled, washed, and cut into thin slices, and the onions peeled and cut into thin slices. Arrange the vegetables and tomatoes in layers; dust a little pepper and salt between the layer, and finish with a layer of potatoes. Cut the butter into little bits, place them on the top of the potatoes, fill the dish with hot water, and bake the hot-pot for 2 hours or more in a hot oven. Add a little more hot water if necessary while baking to make up for what is lost in the cooking.

CABINET PUDDING.

4 slices of Allinson bread toasted, 1-1/4 pints of milk, 8 eggs, 1 oz. of butter, sugar to taste, 2 oz. of chopped almonds, 1 teacupful of mixed currants and sultanas and any kind of flavouring—cinammon, lemon, vanilla, or almond essence. Crush the toast in your hands, and soak it in the milk. Whip the eggs up, melt the butter, and add both to the soaked toast. Thoroughly mix all the various ingredients together. Butter a pie-dish and pour the pudding mixture into it; put a few bits of butter on the top, and bake the pudding for 1 hour in a moderately hot oven.

MENU V.

LEEK SOUP.

2 bunches of leeks, 1-1/2 pints of milk, 1 oz. of butter, 1 lb. of potatoes, pepper and salt to taste, and the juice of 1 lemon. Cut off the coarse part of the green ends of the leeks, and cut the leeks lengthways, so as to be able to brush out the grit. Wash the leeks well, and see no grit remains, then out them in short pieces. Peel, wash, and cut up the potatoes, then cook both vegetables with 2 pints of water. When the vegetables are quite tender, rub them through a sieve. Return the mixture to the saucepan, add the butter, milk, and seasoning, and boil the soup up again. Before serving, add the Lemon juice; serve with sippets of toast or Allinson rusks.

MUSHROOM SAVOURY.

4 slices Allinson bread toast, 8 eggs, 1 pint of milk, 3 oz. of butter, 1 lb. of mushrooms, 1 small onion chopped fine, and pepper and salt to taste. Crush the toast with your hand and soak it in the milk; add the eggs well whipped. Peel, wash, and out up the mushrooms, and fry them and the onion in the butter. When they have cooked in the butter for 10 minutes add them to the other ingredients, and season with pepper and salt. Pour the mixture into a greased pie-dish and bake the savoury for 1 hour. Serve with green vegetables, potatoes, and tomato sauce.

CHOCOLATE MOULD.

1 quart of milk, 2 oz. of potato flour, 2 oz. of Allinson fine wheatmeal, 1 heaped-up tablespoonful of cocoa, 1 dessertspoonful of vanilla essence, and sugar to taste. Smooth the potato flour, wheatmeal, and cocoa with some of the milk. Add sugar to the rest of the milk, boil it up and thicken it with the smoothed ingredients. Let all simmer for 10 minutes, stir frequently, add the vanilla, and mix it well through. Pour the mixture into a wetted mould; turn out when cold, and serve plain or with cold white sauce.

MENU VI.

ARTICHOKE SOUP.

1 lb. each of artichokes and potatoes, 1 Spanish onion, 1 oz. of butter, 1 pint of milk, and pepper and salt to taste. Peel, wash, and cut into dice the artichokes, potatoes, and onion. Cook them until tender in 1 quart of water with the butter and seasoning. When the vegetables are tender rub them through a sieve. Return the liquid to the saucepan, add the milk and boil the soup up again. Add water it the soup is too thick. Serve with small dice of bread fried crisp in butter or vege-butter.

YORKSHIRE PUDDING.

4 eggs, 1/2 lb. of Allinson fine wheatmeal, 1 pint of milk, pepper and salt to taste, 1 oz. of butter. Thoroughly beat the eggs, make a batter of them with the flour and milk, and season it. Well butter a shallow tin, pour in the batter, and cut the rest of the butter in bits. Scatter them over the batter and bake it 3/4 of an hour. Serve with vegetables, potatoes, and sauce. To use half each of Allinson breakfast oats and wheatmeal flour will be found very tasty.

BAKED CARAMEL CUSTARD.

1-1/2 pints of milk, 5 eggs, vanilla essence, 4 oz. of castor sugar for the caramel, and a little more sugar to sweeten the custard. Heat the milk, whip up the eggs, and carefully stir the hot milk into the beaten eggs; flavour with vanilla and sugar to taste. Meanwhile put the castor sugar into a small enamelled saucepan and stir it over a quick fire until it is quite melted and brown. Add about 2 tablespoonfuls of hot water to the caramel, stir thoroughly, and pour it into a tin mould or a cake tin. Let the caramel run all round the sides of the tin; pour in the custard, and bake it in a moderate oven, standing in a larger tin of boiling water, until the custard is set. Let it get cold, turn out, and serve. This is a very dainty sweet dish.

MENU VII.

POTATO SOUP.

2 lbs. of potatoes, 1/2 a stick of celery or the outer stalks of a head of celery, saving the heart for table use, 1 large Spanish onion, 1 pint of milk, 1 oz. of butter, a heaped-up tablespoonful of finely chopped Parsley, and pepper and salt to taste. Peel, wash, and cut in pieces the potatoes, peel and chop roughly the onion, prepare and cut in small pieces the celery. Cook the vegetables in 8 pints of water until they are quite soft. Rub them through a sieve, return the fluid mixture to the saucepan; add the milk, butter, and seasoning, and boil the soup up again; if too thick, add more water. Mix the parsley in the soup just before serving.

BREAD AND CHEESE SAVOURY.

1/2 lb. of Allinson bread, 3 oz. of grated cheese, 1 pint of milk, 3 eggs, pepper and salt to taste, a little nutmeg, and some butter. Cut the bread into slices and butter them; arrange in layers in a pie-dish, spreading some cheese between the layers, and dusting with pepper, salt, and a little nutmeg. Finish with a good sprinkling of cheese. Whip up the eggs, mix them with the milk, and pour the mixture over the bread and cheese in the pie-dish. Pour the custard back into the basin, and repeat the pouring over the contents of the pie-dish. If this is done two or three times, the top slices of bread and butter get soaked, and then bake better. This should also be done when a bread and butter pudding is made. Bake the savoury until brown, which it will be in about 3/4 of an hour.

ORANGE MOULD.

The juice of 7 oranges and of 1 lemon, 6 oz. of sugar, 4 eggs, and 4 oz. of Allinson cornflour. Add enough water to the fruit juices to make 1 quart of liquid; put 1-1/2 pints of this over the fire with the sugar. With the rest smooth the cornflour and mix with it the eggs well beaten. When the liquid in the saucepan is near the boil, stir into it the mixture of egg and cornflour. Keep stirring the mixture over a gentle fire until it has cooked 5 minutes. Turn it into a wetted mould and allow to get cold, then turn out and serve.

A WEEK'S MENU

INVALID COOKERY

BARLEY.

The plants *Hordeum Distichon* and *Hordeum Vulgare* supply most of the barley used in this country. Barley has been used as a food from time out of mind. We find frequent mention of it in the Bible, and in old Latin and Greek books. According to Pliny, an ancient Roman writer, the gladiators were called Hordearii, or "barley eaters," because they were fed on this grain whilst training. These Hordearii were like our pugilists, except that they often fought to the death. Barley has been used from very ancient days for making an intoxicating drink. In Nubia, the liquor made from barley was called Bouzah, from which we get our English word "booze," meaning an intoxicating drink. The first intoxicant drink made in this country was ale, and it was made from barley. Hops were not used for beer or ale in those days. Barley is a good food, and was the chief food of our peasantry until the beginning of the nineteenth century. Barley contains about 7 per cent. of sugar, and its flesh-forming matter is in the form of casin the same as is found in cheese. This casin is not elastic like the gluten of wheat, so that one cannot make a light bread from barley. Here is the chemical composition of barley meal:—

```
Flesh formers 7.5 Heat and force formers (carbon)[A] 76.0 Mineral matters 2.0 Water 14.5 ----- 100.0 =====
```
[A] There is 2.5 per cent. of fat in barley, and 7 per cent. of sugar.

From this analysis we can judge that barley contains all the constituents of a good food. In it we find casin and albumen for our muscles; starch, sugar, and fat to keep us warm and give force; and there is a fair percentage of mineral matter for our bones and teeth.

Allinson's prepared barley may be eaten as porridge or pudding (see directions), and is much more nourishing than rice pudding; it is also good for adding to broth or soup, and to vegetable stews, and is most useful for making gruel and barley water. Barley water contains a great deal of nourishment, more than beef tea, and it can be drunk as a change from tea, coffee, and cocoa. During illness I advise and use barley water and milk, mixed in equal parts, and find this mixture invaluable.

BARLEY FOR BABIES.

Put 1 teaspoonful of Allinson's barley into a breakfast cup; mix this perfectly smooth with cold milk and cold water in equal parts, until the cup is full. Pour into a saucepan and bring to the boil, stirring all the time to prevent it getting lumpy.

BARLEY GRUEL.

Mix 1 large tablespoonful of Allinson's barley with a little cold water, add to this 1 pint of boiling milk and water, boil together a few minutes, take from the fire, let cool, then eat. A little nutmeg gives a pleasant flavour.

BARLEY FOR INVALIDS AND ADULTS.

Use 3 teaspoonfuls of Allinson's barley to 1/2 pint of milk and water, and prepare as "Barley for Babies."

BARLEY JELLY.

Wash, then steep, 6 oz. of pearl barley for 6 hours, pour 3 1/2 pints of boiling water upon it, stew it quickly in a covered jar in a hot oven till perfectly soft and the water absorbed. When half done, add 6 oz. of sugar and a few drops of essence of lemon. 2 1/2 hours is the correct time for stewing the barley, and it is then a better colour than if longer in preparation. Pour it into a mould to set.

BARLEY PORRIDGE.

Take 3 tablespoonfuls of Allinson's barley, mix smoothly with 1/2 pint of cold water, add 1/2 pint of boiling milk, and boil 5 to 10 minutes. Pour on shallow plates to cool, then eat with Allinson wholemeal bread, biscuits, rusks, or toast, or stewed fruits.

BARLEY PUDDINGS.

Take 2 tablespoonfuls of Allinson's barley, mix smoothly with a little milk, pour upon it the remainder of 1 pint of milk, flavour and sweeten to taste, boil 2 or 3 minutes, then add 2 eggs lightly beaten, pour into a pie-dish, and bake to a golden brown. Eat with stewed, fresh, or dried fruits.

BARLEY WATER.

Mix smoothly 2 tablespoonfuls of Allinson's barley with a little cold water, then add it to 1 quart of water in a saucepan, and bring to the boil. Pour into a jug, and when cool add the juice of 1 or 2 oranges or lemons. A little sugar may be added when permissible.

BLACK CURRANT TEA.

1 large tablespoonful of black currant jam, 1 pint boiling water. Stir well together, strain when cold, and serve with a little crushed ice if allowed.

BRAN TEA.

Mix 1 oz. of bran with 1 pint of water, boil for 1/2 hour, strain, and drink cool. A little orange or lemon juice is a pleasant addition. When this is used as a drink at breakfast or tea, a little sugar may be added to it.

BRUNAK.

Take 1-1/2 or 2 teaspoonfuls of Brunak for each large cupful required, mix it with sufficient water, and boil for 2 or 3 minutes to get the full flavour, then strain and add hot milk and sugar to taste. Can be made in a coffee-pot, teapot, or jug if preferred. May be stood on the hob to draw; or if you have any left over from a previous meal it can be boiled up again and served as freshly made.

COCOA.

Put 1 teaspoonful of N.F. cocoa into a breakfast cup; make into a paste with a little cold milk. Fill the cup with milk and water in equal parts, pour into lined saucepan, and boil for 1 minute, stirring carefully. This is best without sugar, and should be given cool.

LEMON WATER.

Squeeze the juice of 1/2 a Lemon into a tumbler of warm or cold water; add just sufficient sugar to take off the tartness. Or the lemon may be peeled first, then cut in slices, and boiling water poured over them; a little of the peel grated in, and sugar added to taste.

OATMEAL PORRIDGE.

Most people, I think, may know how to make porridge; but it is useful to know that if you take 1 pint of water to each heaped-up breakfastcupful of Allinson breakfast oats, you have just the amount of water for a fairly firm porridge. When the water has boiled, and you have stirred in the oats, place the saucepan on the side of the stove on an asbestos mat. Only an occasional stirring will be required, and there is no fear of burning the porridge. If the porridge is preferred thinner, 1 even cupful to 1 pint of water will be found the proportion.

OATMEAL WATER.

This is very useful in cases of illness, and is a most pleasant drink in hot weather, when it can be flavoured with lemon juice and sweetened a little. To 1 quart of water take 3 oz. of coarse oatmeal or Allinson breakfast oats. Let it simmer gently on the stove for about 2 hours. Then rub it through a fine sieve or gravy strainer; rub it well through, adding a little more hot water when rubbed dry, so as to get all the goodness out of the oatmeal. If it is thick when it has been rubbed through sufficiently, thin it down with water or hot milk—half oatmeal water and half milk is a good mixture. Nothing better can be given to adults or children in cases of colds or feverish attacks. It is nourishing and soothing, and in cases of diarrhoea remedial.

RICE PUDDING.

Wash the rice, put it into a pie-dish, cover with cold water, and bake until the rice is nearly soft throughout. Beat up 1 egg with milk, mix with this a little cinnamon or other flavouring, and pour it over the rice; add sugar to taste, and bake until set.

Sago, tapioca, semolina, and hominy puddings are made after the manner of rice pudding.

FOR BABIES.

(*To Prepare the Food.*)

Put 1 teaspoonful of the food into a breakfast cup; mix this perfectly smooth with 2 parts milk to 1 of water until the cup is full. Pour into a saucepan and bring to the boil, stirring all the time to prevent it getting lumpy. It is best without sugar, and should be given cool.

FOR INVALIDS AND ADULTS.

Use 3 teaspoonfuls of the food to 1/2 a pint of milk and water, and prepare as above.

BLANCMANGE.

Mix 6 large tablespoonfuls of the food to a thin paste with a little cold milk, then add 1 quart of milk, flavour with vanilla, lemon or almonds, sweeten to taste; boil 2 or 3 minutes, and pour into wetted mould. Eat with stewed, fresh, or dried fruits, and you have a most nutritious and satisfying dish.

GRUEL.

Mix 1 large tablespoonful of the food with a little cold water, add to this 1 pint of boiling milk and water, boil together a few minutes, take from the fire, let cool, and then eat. A little nutmeg gives a pleasant flavour.

IMPROVED MILK PUDDINGS.

Mix 1 tablespoonful of the food with 1 of rice, sago, tapioca, or hominy, and make as above.

N.B.—The food nicely thickens soups, gravies, &c.

PORRIDGE.

Take 3 tablespoonfuls of the food, mix smoothly, with 1/2 pint of cold water, add 1/2 pint boiling milk, and boil 5 or 10 minutes. Pour on shallow plates to cool, then eat with Allinson wholemeal bread, biscuits, rusks, toast, or stewed fruits.

PUDDINGS.

Take 2 tablespoonfuls of the food, mix smoothly with a little milk, pour upon it the remainder of 1 pint of milk, flavour and sweeten to taste; boil 2 or 3 minutes, then add 2 eggs lightly beaten, pour into a pie-dish, and bake to a golden brown. Eat with stewed, fresh, or dried fruits.

WHOLESOME COOKERY

I.

BREAKFASTS.

As breakfast is the first meal of the day, it must vary in quantity and quality according to the work afterwards to be done. The literary man will best be suited with a light meal, whilst those engaged in hard work will require a heavier one. The clerk, student, business man, or professional man, will find one of the three following breakfasts to suit him well:—

No. I.—Allinson wholemeal bread, 6 to 8 oz., cut thick, with a scrape of butter; with this take from 6 to 8 oz. of ripe, raw fruit, or seasonable green stuff; at the end of the meal have a cup of cool, thin, and not too sweet cocoa, or Brunak, or a cup of cool milk and water, bran tea, or even a cup of water that has been boiled and allowed to go nearly cold. An egg may be taken at this meal by those luxuriously inclined, and if not of a costive habit. The fruits allowed are all the seasonable ones, or dried prunes if there is a tendency to constipation. The green stuffs include watercress, tomatoes, celery, cucumber, and salads. Lettuce must be eaten sparingly at this meal, as it causes a sleepy feeling. Sugar must be used in strict moderation; jam, or fruits stewed with much sugar must be avoided, as they cause mental confusion and disinclination for brain work.

No. II.—3 to 4 oz. of Allinson wholemeal or crushed wheat, coarse oatmeal or groats, hominy, maize or barley meal may be boiled for 1/2 an hour with milk and water, a very little salt being taken by those who use it. When ready, the porridge should be poured upon platters or soup-plates, allowed to cool, and then eaten with bread. Stewed fruits may be eaten with the porridge, or fresh fruit may be taken afterwards. When porridge is made with water, and then eaten with milk, too much fluid enters the stomach, digestion is delayed, and waterbrash frequently occurs. Meals absorb at least thrice their weight of water in cooking, so that 4 oz. of meal will make at least 16 oz. of porridge. Sugar, syrup, treacle, or molasses should not be eaten with porridge, as they are apt to cause acid risings in the mouth, heartburn, and flatulence. In summer, wholemeal and barleymeal make the best porridges, and they may be taken cold; in autumn, winter, and early spring, oatmeal or hominy are the best, and may be eaten lukewarm. When porridges are eaten, no other course should be taken afterwards, but the entire meal should be made of porridge, bread, and fruit. Neither cocoa nor any other fluids should be taken after a porridge meal, or the stomach becomes filled with too much liquid, and indigestion results. To make the best flavoured porridge, the coarse meal or crushed grain should be stewed in the oven for an hour or two; it may be made the day before it is required, and just warmed through before being brought to the table. This may be eaten with Allinson wholemeal bread and a small quantity of milk, or fresh or stewed fruit.

No. III.—Cut 4 to 6 oz. of Allinson wholemeal bread into dice, put into a basin, and pour over about 1/2 a pint of boiling milk, or milk and water; cover the basin with a plate, let it stand ten minutes, and then eat slowly. Sugar or salt should not be added to the bread and milk. An apple, pear, orange, grapes, banana, or other seasonable fruit may be eaten afterwards. No other foods should be eaten at this meal, but only the bread, milk, and fruit.

Labourers, artisans, and those engaged in hard physical work may take any of the above breakfasts. If they take No. I., they may allow themselves from 8 to 10 oz. of bread, and should drink a large cup of Brunak afterwards, as their work requires a fair amount of liquid to carry off some of the heat caused by the burning up of food whilst they are at work. If No. II. breakfast is taken, 6 to 8 oz. of meal may be allowed. If No. III. breakfast is eaten, then 6 or 8 oz. of bread and 2 pint of milk may be taken.

N.B.—Women require about a quarter less food than men do, and must arrange the quantity accordingly.

II.

MIDDAY MEALS.

The meal in the middle of the day must vary according to the work to be done after it. If much mental strain has to be borne or business done, the meal must be a light one, and should be lunch rather than dinner. Those engaged in hard physical work should make their chief meal about midday, and have a light repast in the evening.

LUNCH.—One of the simplest lunches is that composed of Allinson wholemeal bread and fruit. From 6 to 8 oz. of bread may be eaten, and about 1/2 lb. of any raw fruit that is in season; afterwards a glass of lemon water or bran tea, Brunak, or a cup of thin, cool, and not too sweet cocoa may be taken, or a tumbler of milk and water slowly sipped. The fruit may be advantageously replaced by a salad, which is a pleasant change from fruit, and sits as lightly on the stomach. Wholemeal biscuits and fruit, with a cup of fluid, form another good lunch. A basin of any kind of porridge with milk, but without sugar, also makes a light and good midday repast; or a basin of thin vegetable soup and bread, or macaroni, or even plain vegetables. The best lunch of all will be found in Allinson wholemeal bread, and salad or fruit, as it is not wise to burden the system with too much cooked food, and one never feels so light after made dishes as after bread and fruit.

Labouring men who wish to take something with them to work will find 12 oz. of Allinson wholemeal bread, 1/2 lb. fresh fruit, and a large mug of Brunak or cocoa satisfy them well; or instead of cocoa they may have milk and water, lemon water, lemonade, oatmeal water, or some harmless non-alcoholic drink. Another good meal is made from 1/2 lb. of the wholemeal bread and butter, and a 1/4 lb. of peas pudding spread between the slices. The peas can be flavoured with a little pepper, salt, and mustard by those who still cling to condiments. 12 oz. of the wholemeal bread, 2 or 3 oz. of cheese, some raw fruit, or an onion, celery, watercress, or other greenstuff, with a large cup of fluid, form another good meal. 1/2 lb. of coarse oatmeal or crushed wheat made into porridge the day before, and warmed up at midday, will last a man well until he gets home at night. Or a boiled bread pudding may be taken to work, warmed and eaten. This is made from the wholemeal bread, which is soaked in hot water until soft, then crushed or crumbled, some currants or raisins are then mixed with this, a little soaked sago stirred in; lastly, a very little sugar and spice are added as a flavouring. This mixture is then tied up in a pudding cloth and boiled, or it may be put in a pudding basin covered with a cloth, and boiled in a saucepan. A pleasing addition to this pudding is some finely chopped almonds, or Brazil nuts.

III.

DINNERS.

As dinner is the chief meal of the day it should consist of substantial food. It may be taken in the middle of the day by those who work hard; but if taken at night, at least five hours must elapse before going to bed, so that the stomach may have done its work before sleep comes on.

A dinner may consist of many courses or different dishes, but the simpler the dishes and the less numerous the courses the better. A person who makes his meal from one dish only is the wisest of all. He who limits himself to two courses does well, but he who takes more than three courses lays up for himself stomach troubles or disorder of the system. When only one course is had, then good solid food must be eaten; when two courses are the rule, a moderate amount of each should be taken; and it three different dishes are provided, a proportionately lighter quantity of each. Various dishes may be served for the dinner meal, such as soups, omelettes, savouries, pies, batters, and sweet courses.

The plainest dinner any one can eat is that composed of Allinson wholemeal bread and raw fruit. A man in full work may eat from 12 to 16 oz. of the wholemeal bread, and about the same quantity of ripe raw fruit. The bread is best dry, the next best is when a thin scrape of butter is spread on it. If hard physical work has to be done, a cup of Brunak, cocoa, milk and water, or lemon water, should be drunk at the end of the meal. In winter these fluids might be taken warmed, but in summer they are best cool or cold. This wholesome fare can be varied in a variety of ways; some might like a salad instead of the fruit, and others may prefer cold vegetables. A few Brazil nuts, almonds, walnuts, some Spanish nuts, or a piece of cocoanut may be eaten with the bread in winter. Others not subject to piles, constipation, or eczema, &c., may take 2 oz. of cheese and an onion with their bread, or a hard-boiled egg. This simple meal can be easily carried to work, or on a journey. Wholemeal biscuits or Allinson rusks may be used instead of bread if one is on a walking tour, cycling trip, or boating excursion, or even on ordinary occasions for a change.

Of cooked dinners, the simplest is that composed of potatoes baked, steamed, or boiled in their skins, eaten with another vegetable, sauce, and the wholemeal bread. Baked potatoes are the most wholesome, and their skins should always be eaten; steamed potatoes are next; whilst boiled ones, especially if peeled, are not nearly so good. Any seasonable vegetable may be steamed and eaten with the potatoes, such as cauliflower, cabbage, sprouts, broccoli, carrot, turnip, beetroot, parsnips, or boiled celery, or onions. Recipes for the sauces used with this course will be found in another part of the book; they may be parsley, onion, caper, tomato, or brown gravy sauce. This dinner may be varied by adding to it a poached, fried, or boiled egg. As a second course, baked apples, or stewed fresh fruit and bread may be eaten; or Allinson bread pudding, or rice, sago, tapioca, or macaroni pudding with stewed fruit. Persons troubled with piles, varicose veins, varicocele, or constipation must avoid this dinner as much as possible. If they do eat it they must be sure to eat the skins of the potatoes, and take the Allinson bread pudding or bread and fruit afterwards, avoiding puddings of rice, sago, tapioca, or macaroni.

IV.

EVENING MEAL.

Evening meal or tea meal should be the last meal at which solid food is eaten. It should always be a light one, and the later it is eaten the less substantial it should be. Heavy or hard work after tea is no excuse for a supper. This meal must be taken at least three hours before retiring. From 4 to 6 oz. of Allinson wholemeal bread may be allowed with a poached or lightly boiled egg, a salad, or fruit, or some kind of green food. The fluid drunk may be Brunak, cocoa, milk and water, bran tea, or even plain water, boiled and taken cool. Those who are restless at night, nervous, or sleepless must not drink tea at this meal. Fruit in the evening is not considered good, and when taken it should be cooked rather than raw. Boiled celery will be found to be lighter on the stomach at this meal than the raw vegetable. When it is boiled, as little water as possible should be used; the water that the celery is boiled in may be thickened with Allinson fine wheatmeal, made into sauce, and poured over the cooked celery; by this means we do not loose the valuable salts dissolved out of the food by boiling. Mustard and cress, watercress, radishes, and spring onions may be eaten if the evening meal is taken 4 or 5 hours before going to bed. Those who are away from home all day, and who take their food to their work may have some kind of milk pudding at this meal. Wheatmeal blancmange, or cold milk pudding may occasionally be eaten those who are costive will find a boiled onion or some braized onions very useful. Boil the onion in as little water as possible and serve up with the liquor it is boiled in. To prepare braized onions, fry them first until nicely brown, using butter or olive oil, then add a cupful of boiling water to the contents of the frying pan, cover with a plate, and let cook for an hour. This is not really a rich food, but one easy of digestion and of great use to the sleepless. Those who want to rise early must make their last meal a light one. Those troubled with dreams or restlessness must do the same. Very little fluid should be taken last thing at night, as it causes persons to rise frequently to empty the bladder.

V.

SUPPERS.

Hygienic livers will never take such meals, even if tea has been early, or hard work done since the tea meal was taken. No solid food must be eaten. The most that should be consumed is a cup of Brunak, cocoa, lemon water, bran tea, or even boiled water, but never milk. In winter warm drinks may be taken, and in summer cool ones.

VI.

DRINKS.

LEMON WATER is made by squeezing the juice of 1/2 a lemon into a tumbler of warm or cold water; to this is added just enough sugar to take off the tartness. Some peel the lemon first, then cut in slices, pour boiling water over the slices, grate in a little of the peel, and add sugar to taste.

BRUNAK.—Take 1-1/2 to 2 teaspoonfuls of Brunak for each large cupful required, mix it with sufficient water, and boil for 2 or 3 minutes to get the full flavour, then strain and add hot milk and sugar to taste. Can be made in a coffee-pot, teapot, or jug if preferred. May be stood on the hob to draw; or it you have any left over from a previous meal it can be boiled up again and served as freshly made.

COCOA.—This is best made by putting a teaspoonful of any good cocoa, such as Allinson's, into a breakfast cup; boiling water is then poured upon this and stirred; 1 tablespoonful of milk must be added to each cup, and 1 teaspoonful of sugar where sugar is used, or 1 or 2 teaspoonfuls of condensed milk and no extra sugar.

BRAN TEA.—Mix 1 oz. of bran with 1 pint of water; boil for 1/2 an hour, strain, and drink cool. A little orange or lemon juice is a pleasant addition. When this is used as a drink at breakfast or tea, a little milk and sugar may be added to it.

CHOCOLATE.—Allow 1 bar of Allinson's chocolate for each cup of fluid. Break the chocolate in bits, put into a saucepan, add a little boiling water, put on the fire, and stir until the chocolate is dissolved, then add rest of fluid and boil 2 or 3 minutes. Pour the chocolate into cups, and add about 1 tablespoonful of fresh milk to each cup, but no extra sugar. The milk may be added to the chocolate whilst boiling, if desired.

WHOLEMEAL COOKERY

Most of my readers have received great benefit from eating wholemeal bread instead of white, and they may all gain further good it they will use Allinson wholemeal flour in place of white for all cooking purposes. Those who are at all constipated, or who suffer from piles, varicose veins, varicocele, back pain, &c., should never use white flour in cooking. Those who are inclined to stoutness should use wholemeal flour rather than white. Hygienists and health-reformers should not permit white flour to enter their houses, unless it is to make bill-stickers' paste or some like stuff. Toothless children must not be given any food but milk and water until they cut at least two teeth.

Every kind of cookery can be done with wholemeal flour. In making ordinary white sauce or vegetable sauce, this is how we make it; Chop fine some onion or parsley; boil in a small quantity of water, stir in wholemeal flour and milk, add a little pepper and salt, thin with hot water, and thus produce a sauce that helps down vegetables and potatoes. In making a brown sauce we put a little butter or olive oil in the frying-pan; let it bubble and sputter, dredge in Allinson wholemeal flour, stir it round with a knife until browned, add boiling water, pepper, salt, a little ketchup, and you then have a nice brown sauce for many dishes. If we wish to make it very tasty we fry a finely chopped onion first and add that to it. White sweet sauce is made from wholemeal flour, milk, sugar, and a little cinnamon, cloves, lemon juice, vanilla, or other flavouring. Yorkshire puddings, Norfolk dumplings, batter puddings, and such puddings can all be made with wholemeal flour, and are more nourishing and healthy, and do not lie so heavy as those made from white flour. Pancakes can be made from wholemeal flour just as well as from white.

All kinds of pastry, pie-crusts, under crusts, &c., are best made from Allinson wholemeal, and if much butter, lard, or dripping is used they will lie just as heavy, and cause heartburn just as much as those made with white flour. There is a substitute for pie-crusts that is very tasty, and not at all harmful. We call it "batter," and it can be used for savoury dishes as well as sweet ones.

SAVOURY DISHES MADE WITH BATTER.

Fry some potatoes, then some onions, put them in layers in a pie-dish; next make a batter of Allinson wholemeal flour, 1 or 2 eggs, milk, and a little pepper with salt; pour over the fried vegetables as they lie in the dish, bake in the oven from 1/2 an hour to 1 hour, until, in fact, the batter has formed a crust; eat with the usual vegetables. Or chop fine cold vegetables of any kind, fry onions and add to them, put in a pie-dish, pour some of the batter as above over them, and bake. All kinds of cold vegetables, cold soup, porridge, &c., can go into this, and tinned or fresh tomatoes will make it more savoury. Tomatoes may be wiped, put in a pie-dish, batter poured over, and then baked, and are very tasty this way. Butter adds to the flavour of these dishes, but does not make them more wholesome or more nourishing.

STEWED FRUIT PUDDING.

Cut Allinson wholemeal bread into slices a little over a 1/4 of an inch thick, line a pie-dish with these, having first cut off the hard crusts. Then fill the dish with hot stewed fruit of any kind, and at once cover it with a layer of bread, gently pressed on the hot fruit. Turn out when cold on to a flat dish, pour over it a white sauce, and serve.

SUBSTANTIAL BREAD PUDDINGS.

Soak crusts or slices of Allinson bread in hot water, then break fine in a pie-dish, add to this soaked currants, raisins, chopped nuts or almonds, a beaten-up egg, and milk, with sugar and spice, and bake in the oven. Or tie the whole up in a pudding-cloth and boil. Serve with white sauce or eat with stewed fresh fruit. These puddings can be eaten hot or cold; labourers can take them to their work for dinner, and their children cannot have a better meal to take to school.

SWEET BATTER.

Mix Allinson wholemeal flour, milk, 1 or 2 eggs together, and a little sugar and cinnamon, and it is ready for use. Stew ripe cherries, gooseberries, currants, raspberries, plums, damsons, or other ripe fruit in a jar, pour into a pie-dish; pour into the batter named above, bake, and this is a good substitute for a fruit pie. Prunes can be treated the same way, or the batter can be cooked in the saucepan, poured into a mould, allowed to go cold and set; then it forms wholemeal blancmange, and may be eaten with stewed fresh fruit. Rusks, cheesecakes, buns, biscuits, and other like articles as Madeira cake, pound cake, wedding cake, &c., can all be made of wholemeal flour.

WHOLEMEAL SOUP.

Chop fine any kinds of greens or vegetables, stew in a little water until thoroughly done, then add plenty of hot water, with pepper and salt to taste, and a 1/4 of an hour before serving, pour in a cupful of the "Sweet Batter," and you get a thick, nourishing soup. To make it more savoury, fry your vegetables before making into soup.

A MONTH'S MENUS FOR ONE PERSON.

No. 1.

CAULIFLOWER SOUP.

1/2 small cauliflower, 1/2 pint milk and water, small piece of butter, 1 teaspoonful of fine wholemeal, pepper and salt to taste. Wash and cut up the cauliflower, cook till tender with the milk and water, add butter and seasoning; smooth the meal with a little water, thicken the soup with it, boil up for a minute and serve.

WHOLEMEAL BATTER.

2 oz. wholemeal, 1 gill of milk, 1 egg, seasoning to taste. Make a batter of the ingredients, butter a flat tin or a small pie-dish, turn the batter into it, and bake it from 20 to 30 minutes. Eat with vegetables.

BLANCMANGE.

1 even dessertspoonful of wheatmeal, 1 ditto cornflour, 1/4 pint milk, sugar and vanilla to taste. Smooth the meal and cornflour with a little of the milk, bring the rest to the boil, stir in the mixture, add flavouring, let it all simmer for 5 to 8 minutes, stirring all the time. Pour into a wetted mould, and turn out when cold.

No. 2.

ARTICHOKE SOUP.

1/4 lb. artichokes, 1/4 lb. potatoes, 3/4 pint milk and water (equal parts), 1/4 oz. butter, pepper and salt to taste. Peel, wash, and cut up small the vegetables, and cook them in the milk and water, until tender. Rub them through a sieve, return to saucepan, add butter and seasoning, boil up and serve.

FLAGOLETS.

3 oz. of flagolets, 1/4 pint parsley sauce. Cook the flagolets till tender, season with pepper and salt, and serve with the sauce. Make it as follows; 1 gill of milk, 1 teaspoonful of cornflour, 1 teaspoonful of finely chopped parsley, pepper and salt, and a small bit of butter. Boil up the milk, thicken with the cornflour, previously smoothed with a spoonful of water; boil up, season, and mix with the parsley before serving.

WHEATMEAL PUDDING.

2 oz. of fine wheatmeal, 1 egg, 1/2 gill of milk, 1 tablespoonful sultanas washed and picked, 1/2 oz. of oiled butter, a little grated lemon peel, sugar to taste. Beat up the egg and mix well all ingredients; butter a small pie-dish, and bake the pudding about 1/2 hour.

No. 3.

CARROT SOUP.

1 carrot, 1 potato, and 1 small onion cut up small, 1 pint of water, a little butter, and pepper and salt to taste. Cook the vegetables in the water till quite tender, rub them through a sieve, adding a little water if necessary; return to saucepan, add seasoning and butter, boil up and serve.

LENTIL CAKES.

2 oz. of picked and washed Egyptian lentils, 1 small finely chopped and fried onion, 1 dessertspoonful of cold boiled vermicelli, 1 egg, some breadcrumbs, seasoning to taste. Stew the lentils with the onion in just enough water to cover them; when cooked, they should be a thick purée. Season to taste, add the vermicelli, and form into 1 or 2 cakes, dip in egg and breadcrumb, and fry in vege-butter, or butter. Serve with potatoes and green vegetables.

TAPIOCA PUDDING.

1 oz. small tapioca, 1/2 pint of milk, sugar to taste. Put the tapioca into a small pie-dish, let it soak in a very little water for half an hour, pour off any which has not been absorbed. Pour the milk over the soaked tapioca, and bake it in the oven until thoroughly cooked. Eat with or without stewed fruit.

No. 4.

CLEAR SOUP (Julienne).

3/4 pint vegetable stock, 1 tablespoonful dried Julienne (vegetables), a little butter, pepper and salt to taste. Cook the Julienne in the stock until tender, add butter and seasoning and serve.

HAGGIS.

2 oz. of wheatmeal, 1 oz. of rolled oatmeal, 1 egg, 1/4 oz. of oiled butter, 1/2 gill milk, a teaspoonful of grated onion, a pinch of herbs, pepper and salt to taste. Beat up the egg, mix it with the milk, and add the other ingredients. Turn the mixture into a small greased basin, and steam the haggis 1-1/2 hours. Serve with vegetables.

GROUND RICE PUDDING.

1 oz. of ground rice, a scanty 1/2 pint of milk, sugar and flavouring to taste, 1/2 egg. Boil the milk, stir the ground rice into it; let it simmer for 10 minutes, then add sugar and flavouring and the 1/2 egg well beaten; turn the mixture into a small pie-dish, and bake in the oven until a golden colour.

No. 5.

CLEAR TOMATO SOUP.

2 tablespoonfuls of tinned tomatoes, or 1 fair-sized fresh one, 1 small finely chopped and fried onion, a teaspoonful of vermicelli, pepper and salt to taste, 1/2 pint of water. Boil the tomatoes with the onion and water for 5 to 10 minutes, then drain all the liquid; return to the saucepan, season and sprinkle in the vermicelli, let the soup cook until the vermicelli is soft, and serve.

MACARONI WITH CHEESE.

2 oz. of macaroni or Spaghetti, a little grated cheese, pepper and salt to taste. Boil the macaroni in as much water as it will absorb (about 1/2 pint). Season to taste. When tender serve with grated cheese and vegetables.

WHEATMEAL BATTER.

2 oz. of meal, 1 oz. of desiccated cocoanut, 1 gill of milk, 1 egg, sugar to taste, 1/4 oz. of oiled butter. Make a batter of the egg, milk, and meal, add the other ingredients, and bake the batter in a small buttered pie-dish.

No. 6.

LENTIL SOUP.

2 oz. of Egyptian lentils, 2 oz. each of carrots and turnips cut up small, 1/2 oz. of onion chopped fine, 1/2 oz. of butter, seasoning to taste, 1 pint of water. Cook the vegetables and lentils in the water until quite tender, then

rub them through a sieve. Return to the saucepan, add butter and seasoning, boil up, and serve with sippets of toast.

RICE AND TOMATOES.

1/4 lb. rice, 1/2 pint water, 1/4 oz. of butter, pepper and salt to taste, 1 large tomato or two small ones. Set the rice over the fire with the water (cold) and the butter and seasoning; let it simmer until the water is absorbed and the rice fairly tender. It will take 20 minutes. Meanwhile place the tomatoes in a small dish, sprinkle with pepper and salt, place a little bit of butter on each, a few spoonfuls of water in the dish, and bake them from 15 to 25 minutes. Spread the rice on a flat dish, place the tomatoes in the middle, pour the juice over, and serve.

WHEATMEAL AND SAGO PUDDING.

1 dessertspoonful of sago, 1 ditto of wheatmeal, 1/2 pint milk, sugar and flavouring to taste. Boil the sago and wheatmeal in the milk until the sago is well swelled out. Flavour to taste, pour the mixture into a little pie-dish, and bake the pudding until a golden colour.

No. 7.

POTATO SOUP.

1/2 lb. of potatoes, 1 pint of water, 1 small onion, a piece of celery, a little piece of butter, a teaspoonful of chopped parsley, pepper and salt to taste. Peel, wash, and cut up small the vegetables, and cook them in the water till quite tender. Rub the mixture through a sieve, add the butter and seasoning, boil up, mix in the parsley, and serve.

CAULIFLOWER AU GRATIN.

1 small cauliflower, 1 oz. of grated cheese, 1 tablespoonful of breadcrumbs, 1/2 oz. of butter, pepper and salt. Boil the cauliflower until tender, cut it up and arrange it in a small pie-dish; sprinkle over the cheese and breadcrumbs, dust with pepper and salt, place the butter in little bits over the top, and bake the cauliflower until golden brown. Serve with white sauce. (See "Sauces.")

APPLE PIE.

2 medium-sized cooking apples, sugar and cinnamon or lemon peel to taste. Some paste for short crust. Pare, core, and cut up the apples, and fill a small pie-dish with them; add sugar and cinnamon to taste, and a little water. Cover with paste, and bake in a fairly quick oven until brown, then let cook gently for another 1/4 hour in a cooler part of the oven.

No. 8.

POTATO SOUP (2).

2 medium-sized potatoes, 1 small onion chopped fine, and fried a nice brown in butter or vege-butter, 1/4 pint milk, 3/4 pint water, 1 piece of celery, pepper and salt to taste. Peel, wash, and cut up the potatoes, and cut

up the celery. Boil with the water until tender. Rub the vegetables through a sieve, return the soup to the saucepan, add seasoning, milk, and onion; boil up and serve.

SWEET CORN TART.

2 tablespoonfuls of tinned sweet corn, 1/4 oz. of butter, pepper and salt to taste, 1 egg, some paste for crust. Beat up the egg and mix with the sweet corn, season to taste. Roll out the paste and line a plate with it, turn the sweet corn mixture on to the paste, and bake the tart until a light brown. Serve with brown sauce or tomato sauce.

RICE PUDDING.

1 oz. of rice, 1/2 pint of milk, sugar and flavouring to taste. Wash the rice and put it into a pie-dish. Bring the milk to the boil, pour it over the rice, add the sugar and any kind of flavouring, and bake the pudding till the rice is tender.

No. 9.

RICE CHEESE SOUP.

1 dessertspoonful of rice, 3/4 pint water, 1/4 pint milk, 1 oz. grated cheese, 1/4 oz. butter, seasoning to taste. Cook the rice in the milk and water until tender, then add the cheese, butter, and seasoning, and let the soup boil up until the cheese is dissolved.

VEGETABLE PIE.

2 oz. each of potato, carrot, turnip, celery, tomato (or any other vegetable in season), a small onion, 1/2 oz. of butter, pepper and salt to taste, 1 teaspoonful of sago. Chop fine the onion and fry it. Boil all the vegetables, previously washed and cut up, in 1/2 pint of water. When they are quite tender, put all in a pie-dish, adding seasoning to taste. Add enough water for gravy, and sprinkle in the sago. Cover with short crust, and bake in a moderately hot oven.

STEWED PRUNES AND GRATED COCOANUT.

Stew some Californian plums in enough water to cover them well. If possible, they should be soaked over night. Grate some fresh cocoanut, after removing the brown outer skin, and serve separately.

No. 10.

ASPARAGUS SOUP.

1/2 dozen sticks of asparagus, 1/2 pint water, 1/4 pint milk, 1 level dessertspoonful of cornflour, 1/4 oz. of butter, pepper and salt to taste. Boil the asparagus in the water till tender, add the seasoning, and the cornflour smoothed in the milk, boil up and serve.

MACARONI WITH CAPER SAUCE.

2 oz. macaroni, 1/4 pint white sauce (see "Sauces"); 1 teaspoonful capers chopped small, enough of the caper vinegar to taste. Boil the macaroni in 1/2 pint of water until tender. Make the white sauce, then add the capers and vinegar. Serve with vegetables.

PRUNE BATTER.

8 or 10 well-cooked Californian plums, with a little of the juice, 2 oz. of fine wheatmeal, 1/2 oz. of butter, 1 gill of milk, and 1 egg. Make a batter of the milk, meal, and egg, oil the butter, and stir it in. Place the prunes in a little pie-dish, pour the batter over, and bake until a nice brown.

No. 11.

TOMATO SOUP.

1 teacupful of tinned tomatoes, or 6 oz. of fresh ones, 1 teaspoonful of cornflour, 1 small onion, pepper and salt to taste, and a little butter. Chop the onion up fine, and cook the tomatoes and onion in enough water to make 1/2 pint of soup. When cooked 15 minutes rub the vegetables through a sieve; return to the saucepan, boil up, thicken with the cornflour smoothed with a spoonful of water, and add a little piece of butter; serve with sippets of toast.

BREAD STEAK.

One slice of Wholemeal bread, a small finely chopped onion, a little milk, half an egg beaten up, pepper and salt, a little piece of butter. Dip the bread in milk, then in egg; melt the butter in a frying pan, fry the bread and onion a nice brown, sprinkle with seasoning and serve with potato and greens.

SEMOLINA PUDDING.

1 oz. of semolina, 1/2 pint of milk, sugar and vanilla to taste. Boil the semolina in the milk until well thickened, add sugar and flavouring, pour the mixture into a little pie-dish, and bake until a golden colour.

No. 12.

BREAD SOUP.

1 slice of Allinson bread, 1 small finely chopped onion fried brown, a pinch of nutmeg, pepper and salt to taste. Boil the bread in 3/4 pint of water and milk in equal parts, adding the onion and seasoning. When the bread is quite tender, rub all through a sieve, return soup to the saucepan, boil up, and serve.

RICE AND MUSHROOMS.

1/4 lb. of rice, 1/4 lb. of mushrooms, a little butter and seasoning. Cook the rice in 1/2 pint of water, as directed in recipe for "Rice." Peel and wash the mushrooms, place them in a flat tin with a few spoonfuls of water, a dusting of pepper and salt and a bit of butter on each. Bake them from 15 to 20 minutes, spread the rice on a flat dish, place the mushrooms in the middle, pour over the gravy, and serve.

BREAD PUDDING.

3 oz. of bread, 1 oz. sultanas, 1/2 doz. sweet almonds chopped fine, 1 well-beaten egg, cinnamon and sugar to taste, 1/2 oz. of butter, a little milk. Soak the bread in milk, and squeeze the surplus out with a spoon. Mix all the ingredients together, add the butter oiled, pour the mixture into a buttered pie-dish, and bake the pudding from 30 to 45 minutes.

No. 13.

ONION SOUP.

1 small Spanish onion, 1 medium-sized potato, 1/4 oz. of butter, pepper and salt and a pinch of mixed herbs, a little milk. Cut up the vegetables and cook them in 1/2 pint of water, adding a little herbs. When tender, rub the vegetables through a sieve, return the soup to the saucepan, add the butter and seasoning, and serve.

MACARONI AND TOMATOES.

2 oz, of macaroni, 1/2 teacupful tinned tomatoes, 1-1/2 gills of water, a little grated cheese. Cook the rice in the water and tomatoes until tender, add seasoning, and serve with grated cheese and vegetables.

STEAMED PUDDING.

2 oz. wheatmeal, 1 oz. of sago, 1 egg, 1/2 oz. of oiled butter, 1 oz. sultanas, 1/2 saltspoonful of cinnamon, sugar to taste. Soak the sago over the fire in a little water; when almost tender drain off any water that is not absorbed, mix it with the other ingredients, pour the mixture into a soup-or small basin, tie with a cloth, and steam the pudding for an hour. Serve with white sauce.

No. 14.

GREEN PEA SOUP.

1/2 teacupful green peas, 1/4 oz. of butter, 1 spray of mint, a teaspoonful of fine meal, a little milk, pepper and salt to taste. Boil the green peas in 1/2 pint of water, adding seasoning and the mint. When the peas are tender, take out the mint, add the butter, smooth the meal with a little milk, and thicken the soup. Let it cook for 2 to 3 minutes, and serve.

VERMICELLI RISSOLES.

2 ozs. of vermicelli, 1 oz. of grated cheese, 1 egg well beaten, a few breadcrumbs, seasoning to taste, 1 gill of water, a little butter, or vege-butter. Boil the vermicelli in the water until tender and all the water absorbed. Then add seasoning, the egg, the cheese, and a few breadcrumbs, if the mixture is too moist. Form into 2 or 3 little cakes, place little bits of butter on each, and bake them a golden brown.

TRIFLE.

2 sponge cakes, 1 gill of custard, a little jam, a few ratafias, 1/2 oz. of chopped almond. Cut the sponge cakes in half, spread them with jam, arranging them in a little pie-dish, sprinkling crumbled ratafias and the almonds between the pieces of cake. Pour the custard over, let it all soak for half an hour, and serve.

No. 15.

SPLIT PEA SOUP.

2 oz. of split peas cooked overnight, 3 oz. of potatoes cut into pieces, a piece of celery, a slice of Spanish onion chopped up, seasoning to taste. Soak the peas in water overnight, after picking them over and washing them. Set them over the fire in the morning, and cook them with the vegetables till quite tender. Then rub all through a sieve. Return to the saucepan, add pepper and salt, and a little water if necessary; boil up, and serve with sippets of toast.

HOT-POT.

1/2 lb. potatoes, 3 oz. Spanish onion peeled and sliced, 1/2 teacupful tomatoes, 1/2 oz. of butter, pepper and salt to taste. Arrange the potatoes, onions, and tomatoes in layers in a small pie-dish, and sprinkle pepper and salt between the vegetables. Cut the butter in little bits, and scatter them over the top. Fill the dish with boiling water, and boil the hot-pot for 1 to 1-1/2 hours, adding a little hot water if needed.

BAKED APPLES AND WHITE SAUCE.

Wash and core a good-sized apple, fill the core with 1 or 2 stoned dates, and bake it in the oven in a dish or tin with a few spoonfuls of water until well done. Serve with sauce.

No. 16.

LEEK SOUP.

1 leek, 1/4 lb. potatoes, 1/2 pint water, 1 gill of milk, 1/4 oz. of butter, pepper and salt to taste. Peel, wash, and cut up the leek and potatoes, and cook them till tender in the water. Then rub the vegetables through a sieve. Return to the saucepan, add the milk, butter, and seasoning, boil up, and serve.

SAVOURY CUSTARD.

1-1/2 gills of milk, 1 egg, 1 oz. of grated cheese, a pinch of nutmeg, pepper and salt to taste. Proceed as in savoury custard, and serve with potatoes and greens.

CHOCOLATE BLANCMANGE.

1/2 pint of milk, 1 teaspoonful N.F. cocoa, 1 oz. of half cornflour and fine wheatmeal, sugar and vanilla essence to taste. Bring the milk to the boil, mix cocoa, flour, and wheatmeal, and smooth them with a little water. Stir the mixture into the boiling milk, sweeten and flavour, keep stirring, and allow to cook 5 minutes. Pour into a wetted mould, and allow to get cold. Turn out, and serve.

No. 17.

TURNIP SOUP.

1/4 lb. turnip, a small onion, and 2 oz. of potato, a little butter and seasoning, 1/2 pint water. Wash, peel, and cut up the vegetables, and cook them in the water until tender. Rub them through a sieve, return the mixture to the saucepan, add butter and seasoning, boil up, and serve.

POTATO BATTER.

1 gill of milk, 1 egg, 2 oz. wheatmeal, 1 oz. of vege-butter, 6 oz. cold boiled potatoes. Fry the potatoes in the butter, make a batter of the milk, meal, and egg, mix it with the potatoes, add seasoning, pour the mixture in a little pie-dish, and bake the savoury for half an hour.

LEMON MOULD.

1 oz. of tapioca, 1/2 pint of water, juice and rind of 1/4 lemon, 1 large tablespoonful of golden syrup. Boil the tapioca until quite tender, with the Lemon rind, in the water. Take out the rind, add the syrup and lemon juice, mix well, pour the mixture into a wetted mould, turn out when cold, and serve.

No. 18.

APPLE SOUP.

1 large cooking apple, 1 small finely chopped onion, seasoning and sugar to taste, a little butter, 1 teaspoonful of cornflour, 1/2 pint of water. Peel and cut up the apple, and cook with the onion in the water till quite tender. Rub the mixture through a sieve, return to the saucepan, add the butter, seasoning and sugar, thicken the soup with the cornflour, and serve.

RICE CHEESECAKES.

2 oz. rice, 1 gill water, 1 oz. of grated cheese, seasoning, a pinch of nutmeg, 1 egg, a little wheatmeal, and some vege-butter, or butter. Cook the rice in the water until quite dry and soft, mix the egg—well beaten—seasoning, and cheese with the rice, and form the mixture into small cakes. Roll in wheatmeal, and fry them a golden brown. Serve with vegetables and brown sauce.

PLUM PIE.

1/2 lb. ripe plums, sugar to taste, some paste. Wash the plums and put them in a small pie-dish, pour 1/2 teacupful of water over them, add sugar, cover the plums with a short crust, and bake the pie a golden brown.

No. 19.

CELERY SOUP.

1/2 stick celery, 1/2 small onion, 1/4 oz. butter, 1 potato, pepper and salt. Wash, peel, and cut up the vegetables, and cook them in 1/2 pint of water till tender. Rub through a sieve, return to the saucepan, season with pepper and salt, add the butter, boil up, and serve.

APPLE AND ONION PIE.

6 oz. apples, 1/4 lb. Spanish onions, 1 hard-boiled egg, a little butter, pepper and salt to taste, some paste for a short crust. Peel and cut up the apples and onion, stew gently with a little water. When nearly tender, season and add the butter, turn the mixture into a small pie-dish, quarter the egg, and place the pieces on the mixture, cover with a crust, and bake the pie 1/2 hour.

MACARONI PUDDING.

2 oz. macaroni, 1/2 pint milk, 6 eggs, sugar and flavouring to taste. Boil the macaroni in water until tender. Cut into little pieces and place in a little pie-dish; beat the milk, add the egg, well beaten, carefully with it, add sugar

and flavouring, pour the custard over the macaroni, and bake until set. Serve with stewed fruit.

No. 20.

BUTTER BEAN SOUP.

2 oz. of butter beans soaked overnight in 1 pint of water, 1/2 small onion cut up small, 2 oz. carrot, 2 oz. celery, 1/2 oz. butter. Cook all the vegetables until tender, adding water as it boils away. When all is tender, rub the vegetables through a sieve, return to the saucepan, season with pepper and salt, add the butter, boil up the soup, and serve.

SAUSAGES.

1 teacupful of breadcrumbs, 1 egg well beaten, 1/2 small onion chopped fine, 1/2 saltspoonful of herbs, 1/2 oz. butter, seasoning to taste. Oil the butter and mix it with the breadcrumbs, egg, onion, herbs, and seasoning. Make the mixture into sausages, roll them into a little breadcrumb, and fry them brown in a little vege-butter.

ROLLED WHEAT PUDDING.

1 oz. rolled wheat, 1/2 pint milk, 1 tablespoonful of currants and sultanas mixed, sugar to taste. Cook the rolled wheat in the milk for fifteen minutes, then add the fruit, and let simmer another 15 minutes. Pour the mixture into a small pie-dish, and bake in the oven until golden brown.

No. 21.

FRENCH SOUP.

1 small onion chopped fine, 1 oz. of cheese shredded fine, 1 slice of dry toast, 3/4 pint of water, a little milk, pepper and salt to taste. Break up the toast, and set all the ingredients over the fire; cook till the onion is tender, add 1/2 gill of milk, and serve.

VEGETABLE PIE.

1/2 lb. potatoes, peeled and cut in pieces, 1/2 Spanish onion chopped up, 1 tomato, 1/2 oz. butter, pepper and salt, some paste for crust. Stew the potatoes and onion in a little water; when tender, cut up the tomato and mix it in, season and add the butter; place the vegetables in a small pie-dish, cover with paste, and bake 1/2 hour or until golden brown.

CHOCOLATE PUDDING.

1/2 oz. ground rice, 1/2 pint milk, 1 teaspoonful N.F. cocoa, a little vanilla, sugar to taste, and 1 egg. Boil the rice in the milk for 5 minutes, let it cool a little, mix in the egg, well-beaten, cocoa, sugar, and vanilla. Pour the mixture into a small pie-dish, and bake for 20 to 30 minutes.

No. 22.

SORREL SOUP.

1 potato, 1 small onion, 1 good handful of sorrel washed and chopped fine, a little butter, pepper and salt, 1/2 pint water, 1 gill milk. Peel, wash, and cut up the potatoes and onion, boil in the water till tender, and rub through a sieve. Return the mixture to the saucepan, add the milk, sorrel, butter, and seasoning. Simmer gently for 10 minutes, and serve.

SAVOURY BATTER.

2 oz. fine wheatmeal, 1 gill of milk, 1 egg, 1 teaspoonful finely chopped parsley, 1/2 small grated onion, 1/4 oz. butter, pepper and salt. Make a batter of the meal, egg, and milk, mix in the other ingredients, pour the mixture into a buttered pie-dish, and bake the batter 1/2 hour.

STEWED FRUIT AND CUSTARD.

Any kind of stewed fruit. *Custard*: 1 gill of milk, sugar and vanilla to taste, and 1 egg. Heat the milk, beat up the egg, and stir the milk into it gradually; pour the mixture into a small jug, place this in a saucepan of fast-boiling water, keep stirring until the spoon gets coated, which shows that the custard is thickening. Remove the saucepan from the fire immediately, and continue stirring the custard until it is well thickened. Then cool it, placing the jug in cold water. When cold, serve with stewed fruit.

No. 23.

GREEN PEA SOUP.

1/2 teacupful green peas, 1 or 2 finely chopped spring onions, a little butter, pepper and salt, a dessertspoonful of meal, and 1 gill of milk. Cook the green peas and spring onions in 1/2 pint of water until quite tender. Add the butter and seasoning, thicken the soup with the meal (which should be smoothed with the milk), and boil the soup for a minute or two before serving.

MUSHROOM TARTLETS.

1/4 lb. mushrooms, 1/2 oz. butter, pepper and salt, 1/2 oz. vermicelli, cooked and cold, a little paste for short crust. Stew the mushrooms in the butter, after having dried them and cut into pieces. When they are cooked mix them well with the vermicelli. Line a couple of patty pans with the paste, and bake the tartlets until golden brown. Serve with vegetables.

EVE PUDDING.

1 teacupful of breadcrumbs, 1 small apple, peeled, cored, and chopped fine, 1/2 oz. citron peel chopped fine, 1 oz. sultanas, 1/2 oz. oiled butter, 1 egg well beaten, the juice and rind of a small half-lemon, sugar to taste, and a few finely chopped almonds. Mix all the ingredients, pour the mixture into a small buttered basin, cover and steam for 1 hour. Serve with sweet sauce.

No. 24.

MUSHROOM SOUP.

2 oz. mushrooms cut up small, 1/2 small onion chopped fine, 1 dessertspoonful of fine wheatmeal, pepper and salt, 1/2 oz. of butter, a little milk. Stew the mushrooms and onions together in the butter until well cooked, add 1/2 pint of water, and cook the vegetables for 10 minutes. Add seasoning, and the meal smoothed in a little milk. Let the soup thicken and boil up, and serve with sippets of toast.

BUTTER BEANS RISSOLES.

2 oz. butter beans, 1 tablespoonful of cold mashed potatoes, 1/2 small onion chopped fine, a pinch of herbs, 1/2 oz. of butter, seasoning to taste. Soak the beans in butter over night, fry the onion in the butter. Boil the beans in as much water as they absorb until quite tender. Then pass them through a nut-mill or mash them up, and mix with the fried onion, mashed potatoes, herbs, and seasoning; form into little rissoles, roll in breadcrumbs, place them on a buttered tin, place a few bits of butter on the top, and bake in the oven until a nice brown. Serve with vegetables.

RATAFIA CUSTARD.

1/2 pint hot milk, 1 egg well beaten, 1 oz. ratafia broken up, sugar and flavouring to taste. Mix the ingredients, pour the mixture into a small buttered pie-dish, and bake the custard in a moderate oven until set.

CHEESE SANDWICHES.

Cut some slices of rich cheese and place them between some slices of wholemeal bread and butter, like sandwiches. Put them on a plate in the oven, and when the bread is toasted serve on a napkin.

CREAM CHEESE SANDWICHES.

Spread some thin brown bread thickly with cream cheese, then put any kind of jam between the slices; sift with powdered sugar and serve.

CHOCOLATE SANDWICHES.

1/4 pint cream, 2 bars of good chocolate. Grate the chocolate, whip the cream, adding a piece of vanilla 1/2 in. long; slit the latter and remove it when the cream is whipped firmly. Mix the chocolate with the cream and spread the mixture on thin slices of bread; make into sandwiches. If desired sweeter add a little sugar to the cream.

CURRY SANDWICHES.

Pound together the yolks of 8 hard-boiled eggs, a piece of butter the size of an egg, a little salt, a teaspoonful of curry powder, and a tablespoonful of fine breadcrumbs. Pound to a smooth paste and moisten with a little tarragon vinegar.